SOVIET AIR POWER IN TRANSITION

ROBERT P. BERMAN

SOVIET AIR POWER IN TRANSITION

THE BROOKINGS INSTITUTION
Washington, D.C.

Library of Congress Cataloging in Publication Data:

Berman, Robert P   1950–
  Soviet air power in transition.

  (Studies in defense policy)
  Includes bibliographical references.
  1. Aeronautics, Military—Russia.   2. Air power.
I. Title.   II. Series.
UG635.R9B47   358.4′00947   77-86493
ISBN 0-8157-0923-4

9 8 7 6 5 4 3 2 1

THE BROOKINGS INSTITUTION is an independent organization devoted to nonpartisan research, education, and publication in economics, government, foreign policy, and the social sciences generally. Its principal purposes are to aid in the development of sound public policies and to promote public understanding of issues of national importance.

The Institution was founded on December 8, 1927, to merge the activities of the Institute for Government Research, founded in 1916, the Institute of Economics, founded in 1922, and the Robert Brookings Graduate School of Economics and Government, founded in 1924.

The Board of Trustees is responsible for the general administration of the Institution, while the immediate direction of the policies, program, and staff is vested in the President, assisted by an advisory committee of the officers and staff. The by-laws of the Institution state: "It is the function of the Trustees to make possible the conduct of scientific research, and publication, under the most favorable conditions, and to safeguard the independence of the research staff in the pursuit of their studies and in the publication of the results of such studies. It is not a part of their function to determine, control, or influence the conduct of particular investigations or the conclusions reached."

The President bears final responsibility for the decision to publish a manuscript as a Brookings book. In reaching his judgment on the competence, accuracy, and objectivity of each study, the President is advised by the director of the appropriate research program and weighs the views of a panel of expert outside readers who report to him in confidence on the quality of the work. Publication of a work signifies that it is deemed a competent treatment worthy of public consideration but does not imply endorsement of conclusions or recommendations.

The Institution maintains its position of neutrality on issues of public policy in order to safeguard the intellectual freedom of the staff. Hence interpretations or conclusions in Brookings publications should be understood to be solely those of the authors and should not be attributed to the Institution, to its trustees, officers, or other staff members, or to the organizations that support its research.

FOREWORD

Since 1970 the Soviet air force has been modernized and restructured. It is now fitted for a wide variety of missions under various strategic and tactical conditions, including nonnuclear warfare in Europe.

In this study, the eighteenth in the Brookings Studies in Defense Policy series, Robert P. Berman examines the development, composition, utilization, and implications of Soviet air power. He finds that its tactical components, whose primary focus is on Europe, have undergone the most significant change. By the early 1980s, as a result of modernization programs now underway, the Soviet tactical air force is likely to be equipped with multipurpose aircraft capable of attacking NATO airbases and nuclear stockpiles at the onset of a European war. It will thus be able to threaten NATO defenses in a way that it cannot seriously threaten them now; hence Berman concludes that the United States and the NATO powers must improve the survivability of their air and ground forces.

Robert P. Berman is a research associate on the defense analysis staff of the Brookings Foreign Policy Studies program. He thanks Major General Jasper A. Welch, Jr., Air Force Assistant Chief of Staff for Studies and Analysis, and his staff, and Raymond Ennis and Kenneth Huck of the Office of Strategic Research of the Central Intelligence Agency, for their interest and guidance; Benjamin S. Lambeth and Thomas W. Wolfe of the RAND Corporation and Robert E. Weinland of the Center for Naval Analyses for valuable comments; and Harold Berman, Colonel Richard Daleski, Stephanie de Gorog, William Mako, Edward A. Miller, Jr., Deborah S. Slack, Peter D. Walters, and Robert M. Whitaker for their encouragement and suggestions.

He is also grateful to his Brookings colleagues Barry M. Blechman, John C. Baker, and Frederick W. Young for valuable suggestions; to John McWilliams and Penelope S. Harpold, whose efforts minimized the risk of factual error; to Georgina S. Hernandez, Christine Lipsey, and Ann M. Ziegler, who typed the manuscript; and to Alice M. Carroll, who edited it.

The Institution gratefully acknowledges the assistance of the Ford Foundation, whose grant helps to support its work in defense studies. The views expressed herein are those of the author and should not be ascribed to the persons who provided data or who commented on the manuscript, to the Ford Foundation, or to the trustees, officers, or other staff members of the Brookings Institution.

BRUCE K. MACLAURY
President

August 1977
Washington, D.C.

CONTENTS

Appendix Tables

Figures

CHAPTER ONE

INTRODUCTION

Over the years, studies of the Soviet Union's military power have emphasized its capable strategic nuclear forces, its large army, and its newly modernized navy. The most flexible part of the Soviet military, the air forces, has been largely ignored. Because air battles are more fluid and wide ranging than land or maritime encounters, there is a tendency to underestimate the importance of air power and the capabilities of opposing air forces, especially in Europe.

Aircraft, particularly since World War II, have been the key to the rapid increases in overall combat effectiveness and firepower on the modern battlefield. In the United States, for example, the lethality of ground-attack aircraft has increased more than seventy times since World War II, that of battle tanks only about twelve times. And tremendous power can be brought to bear by an air force. A flight of four A-10 ground-attack aircraft can deliver over thirty-six times the amount of explosive that a battalion of eighteen 155 mm artillery pieces can fire in the same length of time.[1]

The United States, Western Europe, and the Soviet Union all consider their air elements essential in both strategic and theater warfare. Before missiles became reliable strategically, aircraft provided a nuclear delivery system for all five nuclear powers. Today, bombers remain an important strategic component for the United States; for the Soviet Union, although they provide a degree of flexibility in nuclear operations, bombers are tailored for conventional roles and theater warfare.

As conventional military capabilities have been given greater emphasis in Soviet military doctrine, tactical air power has become important. Not

1. "Modern Weapons on the Modern Battlefield," TRADOC Bulletin 8 (U.S. Army Training and Doctrine Command, Ft. Monroe, Va.; processed), pp. 3, 17, and 22.

only can an air force be called on to assure the survival of ground or naval forces, but when used properly it can, with its speed, mobility, and concentrated firepower, influence battles decisively.

Politically, air forces can be deftly used to exert pressure over a long period of time. Since they can respond faster in a crisis than either naval or ground forces, and be quickly removed, air units can be used to demonstrate resolve before a political disagreement deteriorates into hostile confrontation. As the United States demonstrated in Korea in the summer of 1976, air forces can be a potent political instrument.

Air forces also reflect a country's technical competence. The United States is beginning to put its fourth generation of tactical jet aircraft (F-14, F-15, F-16, F-18, and A-10) since World War II into service and by the late 1970s will have completed that series. Western Europe is just starting to replace U.S.-designed combat jet aircraft of the second design period (F-104G) with third-generation creations of its own (Jaguar, Tornado, and Alpha), but by the early 1980s will return to a U.S. design for a fourth-generation aircraft (F-16).[2] The Soviet Union still retains first-generation equipment (MIG-17 Fresco), while continuing to produce third-generation models (MIG-23 and MIG-27 Floggers, SU-17 Fitter C, and SU-19 Fencer) and preparing to introduce a fourth generation of aircraft.[3] Table 1-1 shows the development of tactical fighter aircraft in the four ten-year generations of design since World War II.

2. Jaguar is an Anglo-French ground-attack aircraft; Tornado is the multirole aircraft developed by Britain, Germany, and Italy; and Alpha is a light ground-attack aircraft built by Germany and France.

3. Soviet aircraft designators are a conglomeration of Soviet and NATO codes. In the Soviet system, each aircraft is given a design bureau designation (MIG = Mikoyan Gurevich; SU = Sukhoi; YAK = Yakovlev; TU = Tupolev; IL = Ilyushin; LA = Lavochkin) and a number that specifies the design order. For example, a Tupolev bomber of design number 95 is designated: TU-95. When the aircraft is placed in military service, it is also given a military service number (the TU-95 and TU-20 are the same airframe). The NATO code name is given to an aircraft when it is detected by NATO authorities, as a way of describing the aircraft even though the Soviet designator may not be known. The first letter of the code name indicates the type of aircraft: F = fighter, B = bomber, C = cargo, H = helicopter. Jet aircraft are given multisyllabic names (Flogger), propeller-driven aircraft one-syllable names (Cub). Variants of an aircraft type are usually noted either with an abbreviation after the Soviet number (R = reconnaissance), or by a letter after the NATO code name showing a new modification (Fishbed C or Fishbed L). Recent reports indicate that the Soviets may be changing their numbering system, so that an entirely new military number may be given to each modification; SU-17, SU-20, and SU-22, for example, are all variants of Fitter Cs. Design bureaus too may eventually change their names.

Table 1-1. Tactical Aircraft Development, by Design Generation, Selected Countries

Design generation	Aircraft		
	Soviet Union	*United States*	*Western Europe and Canada*
First (1946–55)	MIG-9, MIG-15, MIG-17, MIG-19, IL-28, LA-9, LA-11, LA-15, YAK-15, YAK-23, YAK-25	F-80, F-84, F-86, F-94, F-100, F-101, F-102, F-105, F-106, B-66, F-1H, F-9F, F-6A, F-3B, F-2H, F-7U, A-4	CF-100, SAAB-32, Venom, Canberra, Hunter, Vixen, Sea Hawk, Scimitar, Aquilon, Ouragon, Mystère 4, Vautour 2, Super Mystère
Second (1956–65)	MIG-21, MIG-25, SU-7, SU-9, YAK-28, TU-28	F-4, F-5, F-8, F-11, F-104, A-5, A-6	SAAB-35, Lightning, Buccaneer, Harrier, G-91, Etendard 4, Mirage 3, Mirage 5
Third (1966–75)	MIG-21, MIG-23, MIG-27, SU-11, SU-15, SU-17, SU-19, YAK-36	F-4E, F-111, A-7	SAAB-37, Tornado, Jaguar, F-1, Alpha, Hawk
Fourth (1976–85)	MIG,[a] SU,[b] YAK[c]	F-14, F-15, F-16, F-18, A-10	Mirage 2000, Advanced Harrier, Super Etendard

Sources: William Green and Dennis Punnett, *MacDonald World Air Power Guide* (Doubleday, 1963), pp. 33–34 and 38–43; William Green, *The World Guide to Combat Planes* (Doubleday, 1967), vol. 1, pp. 2–8, 10, 15, 24, 26, 30, 33, 36, 43, 50, 53, 58, 61–62, 64, 67, 70, 72, 75, 78, 80, 82, 86, 90, 94, 98, 101, 201, and 204; William Green and Gordon Swanborough, *The Observer's Soviet Aircraft Directory* (London: Frederick Warne, 1975), pp. 66–70, 77–78, 179, 208, and 210; and *Strategy and Tactics*, no. 53 (November–December 1975), p. 16.

a. Assumes an air combat fighter.
b. Assumes a ground-attack aircraft.
c. Assumes a vertical-takeoff aircraft.

Since each type of aircraft produced is a manifestation of defense requirements formulated some five to ten years before the new model is first flown, combat aircraft are a fairly good indicator of defense thinking.[4] During the last decade, a significant broadening of the Soviet Union's concept of air power became apparent. This study examines the evolution of the Soviet air forces, analyzing the trends in aircraft design and in combat tactics. After suggesting the type of war the Soviet Union will be able to wage through the end of this century, the analysis concludes with

4. Tactical aircraft (fighter-bombers, etc.) have a higher turnover rate than do strategic aircraft (long-range bombers) and may provide greater insight as to design philosophy. They may also reflect technological advancement or product improvement.

a set of recommendations for changes in Western military planning, especially for Europe.

Evolution of the Air Forces

During World War II, Soviet air power did not have the strong influence on Soviet operations that the U.S., British, German, or Japanese air forces had on the military operations of their respective nations. By the time of the German invasion of the Soviet Union, the Soviet air force had seen action four times and should have been an effective force.[5] The purges of the mid and late 1930s, however, are thought to have reduced its officer corps by as much as 75 percent.[6] Designers experimenting with swept-wing and delta-wing airplanes were killed along with generals who advocated strategic bombing. Leadership, experience, and innovation were eliminated. By 1941, Soviet aircraft were generally obsolescent. There was a large number of fighters, but none comparable to the German Messerschmitts or British Spitfires, and the few Soviet bombers could carry only small loads over short distances. No transport aircraft linked together the far-reaching territory of the Soviet Union. There were no early-warning systems. And communications between headquarters and forces in the field were inadequate.[7]

Only in one sense was the Soviet Union truly prepared for war. Beginning in 1935, while plants in the west of the USSR were modernized, new aircraft production centers had been set up east of the Ural Mountains. This insured that some aircraft production was able to continue even when plants in the west were overrun or destroyed.[8]

On the first day of the German invasion in 1941 the Soviet forces, operating under political restrictions, lost over 10 percent of their total inventory of 12,000 aircraft.[9] Defeats marked the Soviet war effort until the battle of Stalingrad, late in 1942. At Stalingrad, the Soviet air force seriously hampered the airborne supply effort on which German ground

5. See Asher Lee, *The Soviet Air and Rocket Forces* (Praeger, 1959), pp. 22–25 and 35–42; Robert A. Kilmarx, *A History of Soviet Air Power* (Praeger, 1962), pp. 151–53; and *The Encyclopedia of Air Warfare* (Crowell, 1975), pp. 56–61.

6. Lee, *The Soviet Air and Rocket Forces*, pp. 33 and 34.

7. Kilmarx, *A History of Soviet Air Power*, p. 187.

8. Ibid., p. 155.

9. Ray Wagner (ed.), *The Soviet Air Force in World War II: The Official History*, trans. Celand Fetzer (Doubleday, 1973), p. 35.

forces depended, and Soviet ground forces overran some forward German air bases. The Soviet air force also was instrumental in destroying retreating German ground units.[10] After that victory the pace of military operations was set by the Soviet forces. During the last German offensive—at Kursk in the summer of 1943—the Soviet air force, with new fighters and better-trained pilots, was able to inflict so much damage on the German air force in so-called independent air operations that soon after the battle the Russians were able to claim air superiority.[11] Other successes followed, particularly in the "right bank" Ukraine, Belorussian, Ylasi-Kishinev, Vistula-Oder, and Berlin operations.

The decisive factor in the air battle after Stalingrad was not, however, any particular tactical breakthrough by the Soviet air force but the withdrawal of a third of the German air force to fight on the Western front. At the same time, Soviet aircraft totals climbed, with the addition of aircraft supplied by the United States or built outside the war zone in the USSR itself.[12] The number of ground-attack aircraft, especially, increased (more than doubling in 1942 alone),[13] and ground-support operations—particularly of the IL-2 Shturmovik units—began to be successful.[14] The size of air operations also grew from a few hundred aircraft per battle in 1941, to a few thousand in 1943, and finally by 1945 in the battle of Berlin to over eight thousand aircraft on call. As important as Soviet growth was the stationing of three-fourths of the entire Luftwaffe in Western Europe for the air defense of Germany when the U.S. and British bombing offensive of Germany began in earnest in 1943.[15] Not only was the number of aircraft in use against the Soviet Union reduced but also the quality of the German planes and their pilots.

During World War II, the United States developed and refined the art of strategic bombing as a main instrument of warfare. The Soviet Union, on the other hand, concentrated on using its air force to increase the striking power of land forces. The Soviet air force had little incentive to

10. Lee, *The Soviet Air and Rocket Forces*, pp. 59–60.

11. Oleg Hoeffding, *Soviet Interdiction Operations 1941–1945*, R-556-PR (Santa Monica, Calif.: Rand Corp., 1970), p. 7; Lee, *The Soviet Air and Rocket Forces*, p. 69; and Wagner, *The Soviet Air Force in World War II*, p. 186.

12. Wagner, *The Soviet Air Force in World War II*, pp. 397–400.

13. John Erickson, *The Road to Stalingrad* (Harper and Row, 1975), p. 557.

14. At the battle of Kursk, for instance, nearly 600 tanks were destroyed in a little over 6 hours by IL-2s. See Witold Liss, "The Ilyushin Il-2," *Profile Publications*, no. 88 (1966), p. 11.

15. Lee, *The Soviet Air and Rocket Forces*, p. 61.

attempt independent missions, such as strategic bombing or deep inter-diction. Nor could it gamble its limited resources on either the innovations in doctrine or the specialized aircraft necessary to carry out such missions. It was committed to the mission that had the greatest applicability for the Soviet army—ground support.

During the war, missions in support of ground forces and missions against German fighters, aimed at permitting the ground-attack units to perform without interference, accounted for two-thirds of the nearly four million sorties undertaken by the Soviet air force.[16] Only about 2 percent of the available aircraft were assigned to defense and even some of these were actually used for ground attack. This was possible because there was no strategic bombing threat to the Soviet Union due to the wide dispersion of Soviet industry and Germany's lack of long-range bombers.

Interdiction operations against the German army also were infrequent, because tactics such as partisan activity effectively tied down a large number of German troops. Long-range bomber and cargo aircraft did drop supplies to partisans, however, both in the USSR and in Yugoslavia.

Occasionally the Soviet air force was able to fly missions that were not devoted to its support of the army. For example, its naval aircraft were moderately successful in disrupting German shipping in the Baltic and Black seas.[17] And on eight occasions, attacks were made against enemy air bases before the initiation of large-scale offensives in western Russia. Other independent missions were also flown in the Far East at the end of the war.

The creation of air armies in 1941 gave much greater flexibility in tacti-cal operations.[18] The air armies always operated, however, under the con-trol of the army front commander; air forces were to "be employed in the framework of joint operations with other arms."[19] Not until early 1942, for example, were bombers and transports separately identified and given a title, Long Range Aviation;[20] their main role, however, remained trans-port.

16. Hoeffding, *Soviet Interdiction Operations*, pp. 5 and 8. Ground-attack mis-sions accounted for 38.1 percent of the sorties and air superiority missions for 28.3; naval aviation missions accounted for 9.1 percent, reconnaissance 8.9 percent, air defense 7.0 percent, deep interdiction 4.1 percent, partisan support 2.8 percent, and other strategic operations 1.6 percent. A sortie is one plane's participation in a mission; a mission may include any number of sorties.
17. Kilmarx, *A History of Soviet Air Power*, p. 198.
18. Ibid., p. 179.
19. Lee, *The Soviet Air and Rocket Forces*, p. 48.
20. Erickson, *The Road To Stalingrad*, p. 376; and translation from *Great Soviet Encyclopedia*, vol. 5 (3rd ed., 1971), p. 3.

By 1943—when there was no longer a serious German air threat—the Russians had largely closed the technical gap in aircraft design with the Germans.[21] By 1944 they could confidently assign ground-attack and reconnaissance missions to the air force in support of their ground forces. But in the end the Soviet air force's legacy included little experience in independent operations in the Western European theater.

The Germans characterized Soviet air activity as monotonous and thought there was exaggerated emphasis on ground-support missions.[22] They noted inadequate training, poor control facilities, faulty reconnaissance operations, and poor workmanship. Soviet operations were hampered by lack of planning, by crude instrumentation, and by lack of air-to-air communications. Strategic bombing and large-scale air-defense operations, which depend on planning and tactical innovation, were largely ignored.

When Soviet forces launched their surprise attack against the Japanese in Manchuria at the end of the war, the air force was able to develop its tactical operations. The experience it gained there in airborne landings and in the transporting of ammunition and fuel by air is relevant to Soviet air activities today.[23] The air forces in Manchuria were responsible for long-range reconnaissance and attacks against command centers, fortifications, supply depots, and railroads. More important, particularly for a modern European setting, they had to develop means of hiding the air power they were assembling to ensure their victory. Surprise, mass, deployment from home bases to forward airfields, and mobility within the war theater played a large part in the successful Manchurian operations. They became a regular feature of Soviet air doctrine over the next thirty years.

In the postwar period, the Soviet air force had to adjust both to rapidly evolving technical achievements and to new concepts of the use of air power in war. Most Western air forces emerged from the war ready to adopt jet propulsion, avionics, the new design techniques, and the types of missiles and nuclear weapons that were developed in the mid and late 1940s. Some of the technological advances were borrowed by the Soviet Union. By 1945, 68 percent of German aircraft production facilities was located in areas occupied by the Soviet army, and German plants were

21. Wagner, *The Soviet Air Force in World War II,* pp. 392–93.
22. Generalleutnant a. D. Klaus Uebe, "Russian Reactions to German Airpower in World War II," *USAF Historical Studies,* no. 176 (Arno, 1964), pp. 90, 95, and 100.
23. John Despres, Lilita Dzirkals, and Barton Whaley, *Timely Seasons of History: The Manchurian Model for Soviet Strategy,* R-1825-NA (Rand Corp., 1976), pp. 61–63.

soon transferred to the USSR. Also, during this period, the Russians purchased British jet engines. From five German engine designs and three British, they were able to develop seventeen engines that they eventually used on thirteen different types of aircraft, including the MIG-15 and TU-16.[24]

With emphasis on consolidation in the early postwar period, the Soviet air force was reduced from twenty thousand aircraft in 1945 to fifteen thousand in 1946.[25] Reductions were made in forces stationed in Germany, Rumania, Austria, and Hungary. By 1956, further reductions were made in the air army based in East Germany.

In the mid-1950s, new requirements were formulated for air defense, mainly in response to U.S. emphasis on strategic nuclear bombing, which had a profound effect on the structure of Soviet air forces.[26] As late as 1975, for example, the basic fighter aircraft found both in the tactical branch of the Soviet air forces and in the air forces of Eastern Europe were designed more for the interception of high-altitude bombers than for combat above a battlefield. As jet aircraft replaced the propeller force, modernization of interceptor and fighter units took priority over long-range strike aircraft.

In the late 1950s and early 1960s, Soviet air power—especially in PVO Strany, the strategic air-defense force—improved markedly with the introduction of a new generation of aircraft. The mission of the Soviet air forces did not change, however. Air power continued to be valued for providing short-range conventional firepower to ground troops and air defense for rear areas. Soviet ground forces, in sharp contrast, began to undergo a major transformation after 1964 from a force geared for nuclear war to a flexible fighting force. The air force having never played a major part in Soviet plans for nuclear conflict did not have to be transformed so radically.

The roles of the air force have changed, however. The appearance in the late 1960s and early 1970s of new military hardware—such as the MIG-23 Flogger B, MIG-27 Flogger D, SU-17 Fitter C and SU-19 Fencer ground-attack planes, the MI-24 Hind attack helicopter, the helicopter cruiser Moskva used for antisubmarine warfare, the aircraft carrier Kiev with YAK-36 Forger vertical takeoff and landing aircraft—marked the

24. Antony C. Sutton, *Western Technology and Soviet Economic Development 1945 to 1965* (Hoover Institution, 1973), pp. 255 and 263.

25. Kilmarx, *A History of Soviet Air Power*, p. 226.

26. Thomas W. Wolfe, *Soviet Power and Europe 1945–1970* (Johns Hopkins Press, 1970), pp. 43 and 47. The first radar warning system in the USSR went up in 1946.

transition of the air forces to a balanced force capable of performing a variety of basic military tasks. The air force today can support new and expanded Soviet concepts of warfare and be used as a weapon of foreign policy in Europe, the Middle East, or other areas of interest to Russia.

Missions of the Air Forces

Soviet air power supports the Soviet military. Two of its missions are strategic—air defense and long-range bombing strikes—and two others —antisubmarine warfare and airlift—might fit that definition. But the latter missions and all of the other tasks assigned to the Soviet air forces are aimed at providing tactical support for the Soviet ground forces or navy in carrying out their missions.

Air Defense. The defense of specific areas against particular threats is a basic mission of any air force. Aircraft used for defense must be capable of intercepting intruders at all altitudes and in any kind of weather. Although they are equipped with radar, Soviet interceptor aircraft depend completely on ground controllers to guide them to the general vicinity of their targets. Soviet defense aircraft include the MIG-17 Fresco, MIG-19 Farmer, MIG-23 Flogger, MIG-25 Foxbat, SU-9 Fishpot B, SU-11 Fishpot C, SU-15 Flagon, YAK-28 Firebar, and TU-28 Fiddler. The Moss, a warning and control aircraft, is expected to detect intrusions into Soviet airspace over oceans. Most nations, such as the members of the Warsaw Pact, that receive Soviet arms use versions of the MIG-21 Fishbed as defense interceptors.

Long-range Air Strikes. Soviet aircraft flying on offensive missions against the United States, Western Europe, or China probably would carry nuclear weapons to be dropped on military, industrial, and administrative targets. These aircraft would have to be capable either of flying very long distances or of refueling in flight. Long-range bombers now in the Soviet inventory include the MYA-4 Bison and TU-20 Bear A and B. Other versions of the MYA-4 Bison can be used to refuel other planes. Medium-range bombers such as the TU-16 Badger A and G, TU-22 Blinder A and B, and Backfire B could be used for strategic strikes directed against Japan, Europe, or China.[27]

Air Combat Support. Combat patrols are necessary to clear the path

---

27. There is considerable controversy on the role of Backfire. See Barry M. Blechman and others, *The Soviet Military Buildup and U.S. Defense Spending* (Brookings Institution, 1977), p. 8.

for aircraft on all other tactical air missions. Whether over land or sea, air combat missions are geared to denying specific areas of operation to enemy aircraft so that ground or naval forces or ground-attack aircraft are protected. In this air warfare, carried out at low and medium altitudes, maneuverability is more important than speed. Squadrons of twelve planes, or even regiments of thirty-six, rather than the few defense aircraft that respond to individual threats, are likely to be used in combat missions (ground control is still strict though). Air combat missions may neutralize a whole theater, as the American air force did at the end of World War II, or, as Soviet doctrine holds, they may control a limited area for specific amounts of time. Soviet air combat craft include the MIG-21 Fishbed J, K, and L and the MIG-23 Flogger B.

Ground Support. While ground units are in combat they can call for air attacks on enemy targets. Their requests must pass through many levels of command, however, and their targets are limited to those designated in the requests since Soviet armies have no forward ground-based air controller, as U.S. forces do, to allow for changes in tactics over the battlefield. There are air liaison personnel in the ground forces and ways to skip echelons, but ground-support missions demand careful coordination to avoid bombing friendly troops or destroying one's own aircraft. Soviet ground-support aircraft include the MIG-17 Fresco, SU-7 Fitter, SU-17 Fitter C, and MI-24 Hind helicopter. Because ground-support missions would most likely focus on targets that could not be destroyed by ground forces, their importance has waned since the recent improvements in the mobility and combat power of Soviet ground forces. They are still important to Eastern European air forces. And it is expected they will be the focus of renewed attention over the next ten years.

General Air Support. Mobile surface-to-surface missiles, concentrations of ground forces, and command and control centers are among the key targets of general air-support missions.[28] This type of battlefield interdiction is meant to restrict the enemy's staying power in battle by making it difficult for him to redeploy his firepower. It would be directed by the front headquarters of a ground operation. Planes used in such missions would operate two hundred to three hundred miles from the edge of the battle area and would have to be able to operate in bad weather. Soviet aircraft best suited for this work are the SU-17 Fitter C, the SU-19 Fencer,

---

28. *Soviet Military Thought,* no. 9, *Dictionary of Basic Military Terms,* trans. Secretary of State Department, Canada, for U.S. Air Force (Government Printing Office, 1976), pp. 61 and 171.

and the MIG-27 Flogger D. Electronic warfare jamming aircraft, such as the IL-28 Beagle and YAK-28 Brewer E, would support these operations as they do most ground-attack sorties.

Massed Air Strikes. Air attacks against launching sites for surface-to-air missiles and air bases and nuclear weapons storage facilities would occur at the outset of a war. These strikes would attempt to establish pathways through the enemy's air defenses, stopping his air force while it is still on the ground in order to achieve air supremacy.[29] Runways, maintenance facilities, and fuel-storage areas would be primary targets. Against aircraft protected by hardened shelters, precision-guided weapons or low-yield nuclear missiles would be required. For use in massed air strikes the Soviet air forces have the TU-16 Badger, TU-22 Blinder, and Backfire, along with the SU-17 Fitter C, SU-19 Fencer, MIG-27 Flogger fighter bombers, and electronic jamming aircraft such as the IL-28 Beagle, YAK-28 Brewer, and AN-12 Cub.

Theater Air Reconnaissance. In preparation for massed air strikes or for long-range missile strikes, theater air reconnaissance describes the general situation in a war zone; it also reports details of the success of combat missions. Such missions require planes capable of flying in all weather conditions, day and night, over the entire area of conflict at all altitudes. Satellites, of course, can assist in this work. The primary Soviet planes that are used for reconnaissance are YAK-27 Mangroves and the MIG-25 Foxbat, which has been used over the Middle East and China[30] (contrary to press reports, it has not been used over Western Europe). The YAK-26 Mandrake, of which only about fifty were built, was used over China and Pakistan but is no longer in service.[31]

Battlefield Air Reconnaissance. Observations in battle areas and assessments of damage after strikes are carried out at low and medium altitudes and often in conditions of low visibility. The information sought by ground-force commanders dictates the missions of battlefield reconnaissance. The MIG-21 Fishbed H is used on these missions.

Airlift Support. Airlifts are used in military theaters to supply critical

29. Marshall of Aviation P.S. Kutakhov, "The Conduct of Air Operations," in *Selected Soviet Military Writing 1970–1975* (GPO, 1976), pp. 240–50, explains in detail how successful independent air operations were in World War II for the Soviet air force. He considers the massed air strike on enemy air bases "one of the most important forms of the struggle for air supremacy."

30. *Aviation Week and Space Technology,* June 25, 1973, p. 11.

31. William Green and Gordon Swanborough, *The Observer's Soviet Aircraft Directory* (London: Frederick Warne, 1975), p. 240.

parts and supplies or to rotate personnel. They can also be used in offensive operations for airborne landings or helicopter assaults. As an instrument of foreign policy, they can be used to move military equipment quickly into countries where a display of power will be effective. The AN-12 Cub, AN-22 Cock, and IL-76 Candid are Military Transport Aviation's major fixed-wing transport aircraft, and the MI-6 Hook and MI-8 Hip its transport helicopters. Various other transports are used for liaison and passenger duties. In time of war, crews of Aeroflot, the civil air service in the USSR, would be pressed into air force service to increase the number of transports in operation.

Antisubmarine Warfare. The great speed of aircraft enables them to search a larger area of the ocean for submarines than ships can in the same amount of time and to respond more quickly to reports of submarine contact. Land-based planes generally have much greater range and endurance than those based on ships and can carry larger crews and more data-processing equipment; they are thus usually more effective. Aircraft based on ships are the KA-25 Hormone A helicopters; those based on land include the MI-4 Hound and MI-14 Haze helicopters along with BE-12 Mail, IL-38 May, and TU-20 Bear F fixed-wing aircraft.

Maritime Reconnaissance and Attack. Reconnaissance and attack missions are responsible, along with satellites operated by PVO Strany, for locating highly valuable targets such as aircraft carriers. In wartime, once they have located their targets, long-range maritime strike aircraft and submarines would attack with standoff weapons. Aircraft used for reconnaissance and attack are the TU-16 Badger and TU-22 Blinder. The TU-20 Bear C, D, and E are used by the air force and navy for reconnaissance only, and the Backfire has also been introduced into the naval air force as an attack plane. At one time MYA-4 Bison Cs, which are still in service with Long Range Aviation, were used as reconnaissance planes by the navy. The BE-12 Mail is used to search for and destroy submarines; since it can carry air-to-surface missiles, it can be used to support small warships in coastal areas.

Maritime Air Support. The Soviet Naval Air Force has recently begun to give the fleet reconnaissance, air-defense, and attack support that in the past could only be provided by land-based aircraft, ships, and submarines. The YAK-36 Forger, which is able to take off and land vertically, provides this support. It was first seen when the Russians deployed their first Kuril carrier, the *Kiev,* in July of 1976.

CHAPTER TWO

STRUCTURE OF THE AIR SERVICES

The Soviet armed forces are divided into five services: strategic missile forces, ground forces, national air defense forces, air forces, and the navy. Both the national air defense forces and the navy have their own air forces. Interceptors are found in PVO Strany, the air arm of the national air defense forces, and maritime strike, reconnaissance, and anti-submarine warfare aircraft are found in the Naval Air Force. The Soviet air force itself is divided into three components: Frontal Aviation, concerned with theater warfare, especially in Europe; Long Range Aviation, the USSR's strategic-bomber force; and Military Transport Aviation, its airlift group.

The Soviet air forces are planned and organized according to unique Soviet perceptions of military needs, based on strict operational or functional requirements. The PVO Strany, along with Warsaw Pact air-defense forces, protects the Soviet Union. Frontal Aviation provides support for the ground forces. Long Range Aviation, Military Transport Aviation, and the Naval Air Force have both supporting roles and independent tactical and intercontinental missions.

The Soviet air forces have developed considerable versatility and depth since the end of World War II, changing from a specialized force focused on defense of the homeland and nuclear attack on Western Europe to a balanced air force that can provide varied and tailored support for naval and ground forces.[1] They can perform long-range strike and reconnaissance missions all over Europe and Asia and adjacent oceans. And they have the ability to reinforce and supply most foreign nations that the Soviet government is seeking to influence politically.

In 1977, there were over 10,400 fixed-wing aircraft and 3,500 heli-

1. Thomas W. Wolfe, *Soviet Power and Europe 1945–1970* (Johns Hopkins Press, 1970), pp. 40 and 47.

Table 2-1. Number of Aircraft in Each of the Soviet Air Forces, 1965, 1970, and 1977

	1965		1970		1977	
Air force	*Fixed-wing planes*	*Heli-copters*	*Fixed-wing planes*	*Heli-copters*	*Fixed-wing planes*	*Heli-copters*
PVO Strany	3,800	0	3,300	0	2,630	0
Naval Air Force	800	200	760	100	940	260
Long Range Aviation	1,075	0	915	0	794	0
Frontal Aviation	3,200	0	3,700	0	4,600	3,000
Military Transport Aviation	1,700	925	1,700	1,600	1,500	320
Total	10,575	1,125	10,375	1,700	10,464	3,580

Sources: Derived from International Institute for Strategic Studies, *The Military Balance, 1965–1966* (London: IISS), pp. 3–5; *1970–1971*, pp. 7–10; and *1977–1978*, pp. 8–10; and from *Allocation of Resources in the Soviet Union and China—1975*, Hearings before the Subcommittee on Priorities and Economy in Government of the Joint Economic Committee, 94:1 (GPO, 1975), pt. 1, pp. 148–49.

copters distributed among the five parts of the Soviet air force (see table 2-1). During the previous ten years the total number of fixed-wing aircraft had remained relatively stable, while the number of helicopters had increased by a considerable amount. But there were major shifts in size among the forces and the emphasis given to each. Both PVO Strany and Long Range Aviation, the strategic forces, were reduced in size, while the general-purpose forces—the Naval Air Force and Frontal Aviation— were enlarged. Transport Aviation has declined slightly in size, but new aircraft designs have significantly increased its capacity.

Ever since their inception, the air forces of the Eastern European members of the Warsaw Pact have mirrored the structure of PVO Strany and Frontal Aviation.[2] Thus, as the Russians relaxed their air-defense requirements, particularly in the south, the total number of aircraft in Eastern European air forces decreased.[3] At the same time, though, multipurpose aircraft were introduced into service which strengthened these Warsaw Pact air armies.

2. Only recently have these countries produced their own aircraft. There have been the Yugoslavian and Rumanian Eagle ground-attack aircraft and two Czech aircraft, the L-29 and L-39. Before the appearance of these models, the only aircraft in Southern and Eastern Europe that were not arms transfers were trainers built on licensed production from Soviet designs. In the Warsaw Pact proper, hardware, organization, and deployments have all been structured to meet Soviet requirements.

3. *Armed Forces Journal*, Aug. 17, 1970, p. 34; and International Institute for Strategic Studies, *The Military Balance 1977–1978* (London: IISS, 1977), pp. 13–15.

Table 2-2. Composition of the PVO Strany, 1977

Type of aircraft	First year in operation	Operating range[a]	Number
MIG-17 Fresco and MIG-19 Farmer	1952 and 1955	Short	250
SU-9 Fishpot B and SU-11 Fishpot C	1961 and 1966	Short	650
YAK-28 P Firebar	1964	Medium	320
TU-28 P Fiddler	1966	Long	150
SU-15 Flagon A, C, D, E, and F	1969–75	Medium	850
MIG-25 Foxbat A	1970	Long	300
MIG-23 P Flogger	1975	Medium	110
Moss	1970	Long	9[b]

Sources: Derived from William Green and Gordon Swanborough, *The Observer's Soviet Aircraft Directory* (London: Frederick Warne, 1975), p. 103; di Carlo Raso, Alf a Tauri, and Pierangelo Caiti, "Le Forze Aeromissilistiche dell'Est," *Aerei*, vol. 4, no. 6 (June 1976), p. 17; and "Military Aircraft of the World," *Flight International*, June 26, 1976, p. 1762.

a. Short-range aircraft have a combat operating radius of up to 400 miles, medium-range up to 600 miles, and long-range beyond 600 miles.

b. Moss, a warning and control craft, is not included in PVO Strany totals in tables 2-1 and 2-3.

Air Defense Forces

PVO Strany, the preeminent arm of the air forces, is responsible for defending military targets and industrial areas in the Soviet Union from air attack. The defense force is composed of some twenty-six hundred airplanes (see table 2-2), a drop of 45–50 percent from its peak strength around 1960. The decline reflects both a recognition that U.S. attack plans now rely on missiles as well as bombers and substantial improvements in every component of the Soviet defense system.

Until the mid-1950s, simply-designed interceptors such as the MIG-15 Fagot, MIG-17 Fresco, and MIG-19 Farmer were used for defense. They were controlled by an unsophisticated ground-radar system and backed up by antiaircraft gun units and the SA-1 Guild missile system around Moscow. The MIG-15, for example, was backed by ground-based controllers whose ground-radar sightings were used to vector the plane into the general path of an incoming bomber. The pilot, lacking airborne radar, depended on visual sighting to close on the target and on cannon to fire on the target. By the late 1950s and mid-1960s, significant numbers of YAK-25 Flashlights, SU-9 Fishpot Bs, YAK-28 Firebars, and SU-11 Fishpot Cs were entering service, although not as quickly as older-model MIGs were being retired. The new aircraft, able to work in any weather, were backed up by a second generation of surface-to-air missiles, the SA-2 Guideline. The MIG-21 also was introduced in this period and served in the Eastern European states' air-defense forces.

Table 2-3. Comparative Strengths of PVO Strany and U.S. Strategic Air Command, 1950-77

	PVO Strany missile launchers		PVO Strany fighters		SAC bombers		
Year	Number[a]	Percent intended for low-altitude interception	Number	Total weight (millions of tons)[b]	Number	Percent capable of low-altitude missions	Number of PVO Strany fighters per SAC bomber
1950	0	0	2,000[e]	21.0	520	0	3.8
1955	[d]	0	4,000	45.4	1,309	0	3.1
1960	4,800	0	5,000	67.3	1,716	10	2.9
1965	8,800	7	3,800	67.8	807	35	4.7
1970	9,700	12	3,300	76.8	501	57	6.6
1977	12,000	33	2,630[e]	88.8	418	82	6.3

Sources: Derived from U.S. Strategic Air Command, "The Development of Strategic Air Command, 1946–1976" (SAC, 1976; processed); Thomas W. Wolfe, *Soviet Power and Europe 1945–1970* (Johns Hopkins Press, 1970), p. 48; Raymond L. Garthoff, *Soviet Strategy in the Nuclear Age* (Praeger, 1962), p. 190; Admiral Thomas H. Moorer, "Report on United States Military Posture for FY 1973" (Joint Chiefs of Staff, Feb. 8, 1972; processed), chart 8; Donald H. Rumsfeld, "Annual Defense Department Report FY 1978" (Department of Defense, 1977; processed), p. 58; and Raso, Tauri, and Caiti, "Le Forze Aeromissilistiche," p. 17.

a. Some 10,000 antiaircraft guns have also been in service.

b. Total weight is a rough measure of an air force's capability. Generally, the heavier an aircraft is, the greater its range and the amount of avionic equipment and air-to-air missiles it carries. Numerous other factors, including the aircraft's design and construction materials, and its engine efficiency, are also important, of course.

c. Not a separate component until 1954.

d. A few were in place by 1955.

e. About 18 percent of the aircraft were capable of low-altitude missions in 1977.

In the late 1960s two long-range, high-altitude interceptors were introduced—the TU-28 Fiddler and MIG-25 Foxbat A. They and the SA-5 Gammon missile were expected to extend the reach of Soviet air defenses far enough to stop Western bombers that might be used to launch long-range missiles. The B-70 bomber, which the United States developed but never produced, and the Skybolt missile, whose development was canceled in 1962, might have played an important part in inducing the Russians to design this defense system. In the same period the SU-15 Flagon, soon to become the standard all-weather interceptor, replaced the early-model MIGs and Sukhois, and the SA-3 Goa missile, for use against low-flying aircraft, began to be deployed. The area covered by ground control was broadened by the introduction of the Moss,[4] an airplane with radar that can detect aircraft over calm water.

Through at least 1970, the USSR heavily favored the air defense forces in allocating its tactical aircraft rubles; no fewer than fifteen of the twenty-one tactical aircraft deployed between 1950 and 1970 were designed to meet the need of defense.[5] In addition air-to-air missiles such as the AA-3 Anab found on the SU-9, SU-11, SU-15, and YAK-28, the AA-5 Ash found on the TU-28, and the AA-6 Acrid found on the MIG-25 all are designed for defense rather than combat missions.

The reasons for this allocation are apparent. The threat of air attack with nuclear weapons became very real to Soviet planners in the 1950s, particularly as the size and quality of the U.S. Strategic Air Command grew. During the Korean War the number of bombers assigned to SAC, which had declined during the previous two years, rose by 50 percent (from 520 to more than 850 bombers), and SAC began to switch from propeller-driven aircraft to jets and to deploy tankers. Although the number of PVO Strany fighters dropped after 1960, Soviet aircraft were becoming far more effective. Yet even in combination with increasing numbers of ground-based missiles, they remained at a disadvantage because of SAC's ability to penetrate defenses at low altitudes (see table 2-3).

In 1954 a reorganization of the Soviet military began that among other things gave the PVO Strany equal status with other services. Air defense was no longer the fragmented responsibility of ground artillery units, naval fighter forces, and Frontal Aviation. But creation of PVO Strany as

4. William Green and Gordon Swanborough, *The Observer's Soviet Aircraft Directory* (London: Frederick Warne, 1975), p. 224.
5. Wolfe, *Soviet Power and Europe,* p. 184.

a separate air force encouraged a drift away from the commonality in design of Soviet tactical fighters. With the increasing threat of the U.S. Strategic Air Command and the U.S. Sixth Fleet, Soviet military planners called for both more complex aircraft and an extensive system of bases and an early warning network to protect the USSR's 37,000-mile frontier.[6]

The 1977 air defense forces are equipped with all-weather aircraft, a sophisticated ground-based radar and reporting system, and air-to-air missiles that are more reliable than earlier ones. Two of the four interceptors introduced into the PVO Strany since 1966 (TU-28 and MIG-25) are high-altitude aircraft, but they make up only 17 percent of the force.[7] They are believed to be intended for use as a first line of defense against late-model B-52s and FB-111s before they drop to low altitudes to approach their targets, and secondarily against reconnaissance aircraft such as the SR-71. The backbone of the PVO Strany continues to be the SU-15 Flagon. These medium-range airplanes—32 percent of the present force —would provide the second layer of air defense. Another medium-range aircraft, the YAK-28 P Firebar, introduced in 1964, and the SU-11 Fishpot C introduced in 1966, make up 24 percent of the force, and short-range older types—the MIG-17, MIG-19, and SU-9—contribute nearly 23 percent. The recently introduced MIG-23 Flogger will probably replace these older models. Total numbers of PVO Strany fighters are expected to rise in the future.

The Soviet Union's air defenses generally are believed to be ineffective against winged vehicles below a thousand feet.[8] Its aircraft perform poorly at low altitudes and its surface-to-air missiles do not do significantly better. The deployment of a modified SU-15, the Flagon E, may be an attempt to plug this gap. The chairman of the U.S. Joint Chiefs of Staff has said that it has a "moderately good intercept capability at low altitude."[9] The MIG-23 Flogger is also suited for low-level operations.

The PVO Strany's most notable shortage has been an interceptor

6. Robert D. Archer, "The Soviet Fighters," *Space/Aeronautics,* July 1968, p. 64.
7. Green and Swanborough, *The Observer's Soviet Aircraft Directory,* pp. 179 and 222.
8. "Statement of Secretary of Defense Melvin R. Laird, Before a Joint Session of the Senate Armed Services Committee and the Senate Subcommittee on Department of Defense Appropriations, on the Fiscal Year 1971 Defense Program and Budget" (Feb. 20, 1970; processed); Defense Program, "USSR Air Defense," declassified material (Feb. 20, 1970; processed).
9. General George S. Brown, "United States Military Posture for FY 1977" (Joint Chiefs of Staff, Jan. 20, 1976; processed), p. 44.

system that would enable high-flying aircraft to detect low-flying bombers and destroy them with "shoot-down" missiles. Western observers, having for years expected such a development, thought that was the MIG-25 Foxbat A's role, but its radar signature suggests that is not so.[10] The Moss, an airborne warning and control craft, can discriminate between targets and the background over water, but not over land. Moreover, both Moss and Foxbat may be handicapped by poor data-processing systems. In the future a long-range aircraft with high endurance, but not necessarily high supersonic speed, armed with air-to-air missiles may be needed as a counter to aircraft armed with cruise missiles.

Twelve thousand surface-to-air missile launchers are coordinated with the PVO Strany fighter units.[11] In the 1950s more than 3,000 launchers for SA-1 Guild high-altitude missiles were set in two rings around Moscow, and over 5,000 launchers for SA-2 Guideline missiles were put in service by 1967,[12] most of them west of the Ural Mountains but a few in the Far East. The SA-1s and SA-2s are being supplanted by the SA-3 Goa and the SA-5 Gammon systems, introduced in 1961 and 1967. There were about 300 sites for the low-altitude SA-3 Goa missile in the western USSR and near China in 1976.[13] An average of 25 sites has been added each year since 1969. Newer versions of the SA-3 may be more effective than earlier models. In 1976 there were also 105–110 sites for the long-range, high-altitude SA-5 Gammons,[14] each with up to 18 launchers.[15] They were being built from 1969 to 1976 at a rate of almost seven per year. By the early 1980s there is also likely to be a new low-level air-defense missile introduced.

Despite the improvements in PVO Strany since its modernization programs began in 1964, it is still vulnerable to the U.S. bomber force. The chairman of the U.S. Joint Chiefs of Staff estimated in 1974 that 70–80 percent of the attacking U.S. bomber force would reach their targets.[16] If

10. "Mig 25 Signals Suggest Recon Role," *Aviation Week and Space Technology*, Jan. 27, 1975, p. 61.

11. IISS, *The Military Balance 1977–1978*, p. 8.

12. "Statement of Secretary of Defense Laird," p. 61.

13. *Full Committee Consideration of Overall National Security Program and Related Budget Requirements*, House Armed Services Committee, 94:1 (GPO, 1976), pp. 133–34.

14. *Newsweek,* Feb. 9, 1976, p. 13.

15. "Statement of Secretary of Defense Clark M. Clifford, declassified material. The Fiscal Year 1970–74 Defense Program and 1970 Defense Budget" (Jan. 13, 1969; processed), p. 86–87.

16. *Washington Post,* Mar. 23, 1974.

further developments of Soviet missiles and aircraft are to be effective, they will have to focus on countering the threat posed by the introduction of the cruise missile and the maintaining of late-model B-52s in the U.S. bomber force.

The Naval Air Force

The Naval Air Force is designed to provide combat support to the Soviet navy. Within the navy it has a certain degree of autonomy. The force, whose composition over two decades is shown in table 2-4, is mainly shore-based, although helicopters are stationed aboard the large antisubmarine cruisers of the Moskva, Kresta, and Kara classes, and vertical takeoff aircraft on the Kuril carriers.

In the event of either a conventional war or an all-out nuclear exchange, the navy's targets would include valuable units such as aircraft carriers. Groups of twenty to thirty strike aircraft would carry out attacks in conjunction with submarines armed with missiles and certain surface ships. These forces would pose a complex problem for U.S. carrier task forces. Antisubmarine aircraft would try to halt nuclear attack submarines threatening the Soviet navy's Yankee and Delta submarines, which are armed with ballistic missiles, and in certain areas might also attempt to destroy Western submarines equipped with ballistic missiles.

The Naval Air Force in the 1950s had primary responsibility for the air defense of coastal areas and harbors, a duty that absorbed one-half of its resources. Its basic aircraft were the MIG-15 and MIG-17 day fighters. In the mid-1950s responsibility for air defense was transferred to the PVO Strany as part of the general reorganization of the Soviet military. The navy at this time also had in service TU-14 Bosuns and IL-28 Beagles, medium-range torpedo bombers that could strike at Western amphibious units, and TU-4 Bulls for attacking harbor installations.[17] Together they made up almost one-third of the force. In the late fifties when aircraft carriers came to be seen as a major threat as a base for nuclear strikes against the Soviet homeland, the Naval Air Force began a major shift to long-range aircraft that could operate far out at sea. Since the mid-1960s up to a third of the navy's aircraft have been designated for work against carriers. TU-16 Badgers, some equipped for reconnaissance and others for

17. Siegfried Breyer, *Guide to the Soviet Navy* (U.S. Naval Institute, 1970), p. 10.

Table 2-4. Composition of the Soviet Naval Air Force, 1955, 1965, and 1977

Type of aircraft	1955		1965		1977	
	Number	Percent	Number	Percent	Number	Percent
Fighters and fighter-bombers (MIG-15, MIG-17, SU-17)	2,000	50	0	0	40	3
Torpedo bombers (TU-14, IL-28)	1,000	25	100	11	0	0
Medium bombers with anti-ship missiles (TU-16, TU-22, Backfire)	0	0	250	28	315	26
Medium bombers (TU-4, TU-16, TU-22)	250	6	50	6	48	4
Multipurpose aircraft (YAK-36)	0	0	0	0	30	3
Reconnaissance, electronic warfare, and tanker aircraft (TU-4, TU-16, TU-20)	240	6	140	16	194	16
Antisubmarine aircraft (BE-6, BE-12, IL-38, TU-20)	60	2	60	7	160	13
Antisubmarine helicopters	0	0	100	11	260	22
Other aircraft	450	11	200	22	153	13
Total	4,000	100	900	100	1,200	100

Sources: Derived from "Soviet Naval Air Force: 1965–1975," *Sea Power*, vol. 19, no. 5 (May 1976); M. G. Saunders, ed., *The Soviet Navy* (Praeger, 1958), p. 191; and IISS, *The Military Balance 1977–1978*, p. 9. Percentages may not add to 100 because of rounding.

strikes with missiles, began to enter the inventory by 1959. The TU-16 Badger could carry over twelve times the offensive load that earlier Soviet naval aircraft such as the IL-28 could. Among the indications of aviation's significant place in the restructured Soviet navy was the initiation in 1963 of TU-16 flights over U.S. aircraft carriers in transit as well as at their known combat patrol locations.[18] Twelve years later, when the Soviet navy conducted a major worldwide fleet exercise (Vesna), seven hundred aircraft sorties of all kinds were flown over a fourteen-day period by both Naval Air Force and Long Range Aviation units.

To help fill the requirement for greater flexibility, the Naval Air Force also began to add TU-20 Bear D and KA-25 Hormone B helicopters, which provide midcourse guidance for long-range missiles launched from

18. Norman Polmar, *Aircraft Carriers* (Doubleday, 1969), p. 662–63. Long Range Aviation's Bears began carrier overflights earlier than this.

submarines or surface ships. In 1977, 16 percent of the force was assigned to these support functions, as opposed to 6 percent in the mid-1950s.

In the early 1960s, the TU-22 Blinder C, a short-range bomber capable of approaching its target at supersonic speeds, was introduced in small numbers.[19] Deployments began to the Black Sea Fleet in 1968 as additional counters to Sixth Fleet carriers. The Backfire is now being introduced into Soviet naval aviation; it can fly faster than the TU-22 Blinder and carry a payload as large as the TU-16 Badger almost twice the distance.[20] With these three planes the Soviet Naval Air Force has more than four times the offensive power it could mass against ships in 1955.[21] The Backfire, built for both strike and reconnaissance missions, symbolizes the transformation of the Naval Air Force from a modest force to one able to carry out varied missions at great distances.

Other types of aircraft being deployed to the navy include the SU-17 Fitter, a ground-attack aircraft assigned to the Baltic fleet; it would provide general air and ground support for the naval infantry brigade operating there in wartime. It is likely to show up in other areas like the Black Sea also. Naval infantry brigades may also be supported by Hind helicopters in coastal operations.

From a rather insignificant role during the 1950s and 1960s, antisubmarine warfare has become increasingly important as the Americans, British, and French have deployed submarines that could attack both land and naval targets. In the mid-1960s only 15 percent of the force was devoted to antisubmarine duty; 35 percent now has this assignment. The Soviet navy, initially equipped with BE-6 Madge flying boats developed in 1949, began in 1965 to deploy the short-range BE-12 Mail seaplanes for use against submarines.[22] The Bear F and the IL-38 May patrol aircraft introduced in 1970 greatly expanded the open ocean areas that could be searched for submarines.[23] They carry equipment for determining the area submarines are in (though not for exact detection and classification) and weapons for killing submarines. The low numbers in service raise some doubts about their capability, however. If sensor technology is improved, a new model of the May, produced in larger numbers, is possible. Since

19. Green and Swanborough, *The Observer's Soviet Aircraft Directory*, p. 219.

20. Georg Panyalev, "Backfire—Soviet Counter to American B-1," *International Defense Review*, vol. 8 (May 1975), pp. 640–41.

21. A calculation based on the maximum combat radius and maximum payload of aircraft in the inventory.

22. Green and Swanborough, *The Observer's Soviet Aircraft Directory*, p. 91.

23. Ibid., p. 93.

1967 the KA-25 Hormone A helicopter, which can search ocean areas in a hundred-mile radius of its home base, has been operating from sea as well as land bases.[24] It can relay information to antisubmarine ships sailing nearby. A new sea-based helicopter for antisubmarine work is likely to be introduced, possibly in conjunction with a new surface ship.

With the introduction of the Kuril-class aircraft carrier *Kiev* in the summer of 1976, more helicopters became available at sea.[25] The *Kiev* also carried the navy's first fixed-wing sea-based aircraft, the Forger, which is similar to the U.S. Marine Corps and Royal Air Force Harrier, although larger. It seems likely to be a multipurpose aircraft, conceivably to be used for air combat, reconnaissance, and strikes against enemy antisubmarine units. (For a description of Soviet carriers and their aircraft, see appendix A.)

Today, the Soviet Naval Air Force has about 1,200 aircraft in its inventory, an increase of 33 percent over 1965. Of these, about 70 percent are assigned for operations in a NATO war to the Northern Fleet, based on the Kola peninsula, the Baltic Fleet, and the Black Sea Fleet.[26] The primary plane, making up 36 percent of the aircraft is the TU-16 Badger B, C, D, E, F, and G, in strike, reconnaissance, electronic warfare, and tanker versions. It is expected to be replaced gradually by the Backfire, but this modernization is not likely to be completed until well into the 1980s.

For long-range reconnaissance, missile guidance, and antisubmarine duties, Bear D and F models are used. Although they make up only 5 percent of the force, they have a greater range than any other naval plane. While an old design, these are not obsolete aircraft; naval versions were produced until 1971.[27] About 6 percent of the force is now made up of Forgers, the multipurpose aircraft that can take off and land vertically, and SU-17 Fitter Cs, which are ground-attack aircraft. The Fitter is expected to be able to increase the amount of fire support available to the naval infantry as older gun-armed destroyers are retired. Against submarines, BE-12 Mail, IL-38 May, and Bear F fixed-wing aircraft and KA-25 Hormone, MI-4 Hound, and MI-14 Haze helicopters are used.

24. Ibid., p. 154.

25. "Aircraft Carrier Joins Soviet Fleet," *Washington Post,* July 19, 1976.

26. Admiral Thomas H. Moorer, "United States Military Posture for FY 1974" (Joint Chiefs of Staff, Mar. 26, 1973; processed), p. 53.

27. *Allocation of Resources in the Soviet Union and China—1976,* Hearings before the Subcommittee on Priorities and Economy in Government of the Joint Economic Committee, 94:2 (GPO, 1976), p. 69.

In addition, a few MI-8 Hips are available for mine-spotting and AN-12 Cubs for electronic intelligence work. Naval Air units equipped with Badgers and Long Range Aviation units with Bear Cs and Es coordinate both their training and operations in open ocean surveillance and strike duties.

Although the Naval Air Force has been largely dependent on the regular air force for its equipment in the past, that too is changing. The BE-12 Mail, IL-38 May, and KA-25 Hormone have all been designed to meet specific naval requirements. Such exotic air platforms as the experimental Ekranoplan, possibly intended for regional antisubmarine work, would continue this pattern (this "Caspian Sea monster" uses gas turbines in both takeoff and cruising). With the introduction of aircraft carriers and the specialized fixed-wing aircraft, like the YAK-36 Forger, that must be operated from them, this independent trend is likely to continue.

The Soviet Naval Air Force is bringing into balance the type of support that it can best give to the navy and its overall mission: ensuring control of regional waters (with the Fitter, Mail, Hound, and Haze), countering enemy forward-based systems such as the aircraft carrier (with Backfire, Badger, Bear, and Blinder), and improving its ability to protect its own strategic submarines (with May, Bear F, Hormone, and Forger).

Long Range Aviation

Long-range and strategic air attacks, predominantly over Europe or China, are the responsibility of Long Range Aviation. Its missions could be flown independently of a land battle and could involve either nuclear or conventional weapons. Long Range Aviation also gathers intelligence and provides air support for Soviet naval operations. It has had a fair degree of autonomy within the Soviet air force in the postwar period.

Because aircraft may have assumed less importance in Soviet strategic planning, Long Range Aviation has changed the least of all the Soviet air forces (table 2-5). Its first bomber, the TU-4 Bull, was a medium-range, propeller-driven copy of the U.S. B-29, which entered service in 1948[28] and was directed at targets in Europe. Soviet planners found it much more efficient and credible to aim nuclear weapons at Europe than to tackle the problem of reaching targets in the United States, which would make more demands on the aircraft, require refueling in flight, and call for different types of pilot training.[29]

28. Green and Swanborough, *The Observer's Soviet Aircraft Directory*, p. 29.
29. Wolfe, *Soviet Power and Europe*, p. 40.

Table 2-5. Numbers and Types of Bombers and Tankers Assigned to Long Range Aviation, 1950-77

Year	Medium-range aircraft		Long-range aircraft	
	Type	Number	Type	Number
1950	TU-4 Bull	900[a]	...	...
1955	TU-4 Bull	400	...	...
	TU-16 Badger	600	...	...
1960	TU-16 Badger	1,000	TU-20 Bear	100
			MYA-4 Bison	35
1965	TU-16 Badger	775	TU-20 Bear	110
	TU-22 Blinder	105	MYA-4 Bison	85[b]
1970	TU-16 Badger	550	TU-20 Bear	110
	TU-22 Blinder	175	MYA-4 Bison	85[b]
1977	TU-16 Badger	430[c]	TU-20 Bear	104[d]
	TU-22 Blinder	146[e]	MYA-4 Bison	79[f]
	Backfire	35	...	...

Sources: Derived from "Statement of Secretary of Defense Melvin R. Laird Before a Joint Session of the Senate Armed Services Committee and the Senate Subcommittee on Department of Defense Appropriations, on the Fiscal Year 1971 Defense Program and Budget" (Feb. 20, 1970; processed), pp. 57–58; Green and Swanborough, *The Observer's Soviet Aircraft Directory*, p. 29; IISS, *The Military Balance 1977–1978*, p. 8; and "United States Military Posture for FY 1978, Chairman of the Joint Chiefs of Staff, General George S. Brown" (Jan. 20, 1977; processed), p. 19.

a. Assumes production began in 1947 and ended with 1,500 aircraft for both Long Range Aviation and the Naval Air Force in 1953.

b. Includes 50 tankers.

c. Includes 9 tankers, 22 reconnaissance aircraft, and 94 electronic warfare aircraft.

d. Includes 4 reconnaissance aircraft.

e. Includes 10 reconnaissance aircraft.

f. Includes 44 tankers.

Between 1952 and 1954 three planes were tested as replacements for the TU-4s, whose deficiencies became obvious in the daylight bombing missions of the B-29s over North Korea.[30] The TU-16 Badger A, an all-jet medium bomber, was selected as the replacement and put in service in 1954. Its selection again emphasized that for the Soviet Union the major targets in a nuclear strike by aircraft would be Western Europe and U.S. bases in Britain, Spain, and North Africa.

Introduction of small numbers of the longer-range MYA-4 Bison and of the TU-20 Bear A in 1956 and 1957 did give Long Range Aviation a limited means of striking at the United States. Though this "token intercontinental threat," as Thomas W. Wolfe described it, reached a peak by the mid-1960s of about two hundred bombers and tankers,[31] it caused the United States to make large expenditures for air defense.[32] Only one new

30. "Mig 15 Dims USAF's A-Bomb Hopes," *Aviation Week and Space Technology,* Feb. 4, 1952, p. 16.

31. "Statement of Secretary of Defense Laird," p. 57.

32. Strobe Talbott, ed., *Khrushchev Remembers: The Last Testament* (Little, Brown, 1974), pp. 40 and 41.

Table 2-6. Characteristics of Soviet Medium-range Bombers

Characteristic	TU-4 Bull	TU-16 Badger	TU-22 Blinder	Backfire
Maximum speed (Mach number)	0.4	0.9	1.5	2.0
Combat radius (miles)[a]	1,670	1,900	2,000	900–2,750[b]
Weight (tons)	70.0	85.0	92.5	115.5
Ordnance load (tons)	5	10	6	10
Standoff weapons[c]	0	2 AS-5 or AS-6	1 AS-4[d]	1 AS-4 or 2 AS-6
Defensive weapons	12 guns	6 cannon (23 mm) and jamming equipment	1 cannon (23 mm) and jamming equipment	1 cannon (37 mm) and advanced jamming equipment

Sources: Green and Swanborough, *The Observer's Soviet Aircraft Directory*, pp. 29, 212, 219, and 225; R. Meller, "Europe's New Generation of Combat Aircraft," *International Defense Review*, vol. 8 (April 1975), p. 181; and *Flight International*, Mar. 5, 1977, p. 576.

a. Engines are designed for efficient operation at low altitude or for cruising at high altitude, but not for both.

b. Flying at low altitudes, the plane has an operating radius of 900 miles, but at high altitudes of 2,750 miles. Flying in transit at high altitudes and over its target at low altitudes, its radius is 1,900 miles.

c. Typical load of air-to-surface missiles.

d. Units with Naval Air Force reportedly carry conventional bombs.

long-range heavy Soviet bomber (150 tons and over) has been tested since the first Bear flight in 1954. This was the MYA M-50 Bounder. It is possible that this aircraft was a competitor of the Bear but was slowed in development by technical problems. It offered additional speed but lacked range. There have been hints since 1974 that a Bear replacement may be forthcoming in the 1980s.

By 1959 the Soviets were testing a supersonic bomber, the TU-22 Blinder A.[33] It could fly at very high speeds, but so briefly that it was dismissed as a potential replacement for the TU-16. A few Blinders were added to Long Range Aviation, however.

In 1969, flight testing began on another medium-range bomber, the Backfire. The Backfire B now being phased into service has greater range and endurance than its predecessors, and superior electronic counter-measures. This ensures flexibility in covering European targets, not to mention extending maritime coverage. When traveling medium distances, the Backfire can fly relatively fast and at relatively low altitudes. If it is to make intercontinental trips, however, without tanker support, the aircraft would have to fly at high altitudes and relatively slowly, as table 2-6 shows.

33. Green and Swanborough, *The Observer's Soviet Aircraft Directory*, pp. 219 and 221.

By the late 1970s, Long Range Aviation (and the Naval Air Force) will be facing a problem of block obsolescence as the TU-16s, the backbone of their strike forces, become due for retirement. With 1,800 Badgers built over a six-year period beginning about 1953, and assuming a twenty-year lifetime (probably generous, considering that TU-22s were being investigated for this role eighteen years ago), large numbers of new medium-range aircraft will be required. About 350 Backfires are expected to be built for Long Range Aviation by the mid-1980s, and about 100 for the navy.[34]

At present, Long Range Aviation has about fifty tankers to support medium and heavy bomber missions. They are based on older designs of the TU-16 and MYA-4 and eventually will have to be replaced, perhaps by later-model MYA-4 Bisons, TU-16 Badgers, or a modification of the IL-76 Candid cargo aircraft. Additional tankers would add flexibility and increase the coverage of Long Range operations, and they could support Naval Air Force operations. They could also be used to refuel Frontal Aviation's Fencers and PVO Strany's late-model Foxbats.

As best can be discerned, much of the Soviet air forces' investment in air-to-ground weapons has been concentrated in Long Range Aviation and the Naval Air Force. Between 1961 and 1976 six different types of standoff, air-to-surface missiles were observed.[35] A few are similar in airframe construction to jet fighters, like the MIG-15 and MIG-19, and can carry nuclear or conventional explosives (see table 2-7). Aircraft armed with these weapons can stay out of range of ground- or sea-based air-defense systems. Moreover, standoff weapons can be used against enemy defenses, thus extending the life of a bomber by sparing it from metal-wrenching, low-altitude evasion tactics. They may have been adopted to keep bombers in service in an all-missile era.

Frontal Aviation

The Soviet tactical air arm, Frontal Aviation, is responsible for supporting the ground forces in combat areas, through air combat and ground

34. "Air Power for the Pact," *Flight International*, June 5, 1976, p. 1513. Bears too will be on the decline, with only 80 expected in service by 1980.

35. Michael J. H. Taylor and John W. R. Taylor, *Missiles of the World* (Scribner, 1972), pp. 61–63; and Panyalev, "Backfire—Soviet Counter to American B-1," p. 641.

Table 2-7. Characteristics of Soviet Standoff Air-to-Surface Weapons

Characteristic	AS-1 Kennel	AS-2 Kipper	AS-3 Kangaroo	AS-4 Kitchen	AS-5 Kelt	AS-6 Kingfish
Range (miles)	60	115	317	185–290[a]	140	135–345[a]
Speed (Mach number)	0.9	1.4	1.8	3.5	1.2	3.0
Type of warhead	High explosive	High explosive or nuclear	Nuclear	Nuclear	High explosive or nuclear	Nuclear
Guidance	Radio command	Radar homing[b]	Radar command[b]	Radar homing	Radar homing	Inertial
Launch vehicle	Badger B	Badger C	Bear B[c]	Blinder	Badger G	Backfire B
Mission	Antishipping	Antishipping	Area destruction	Multipurpose	Antishipping, antiradar	Multipurpose

Sources: Michael J. H. Taylor and John W. R. Taylor, *Missiles of the World* (Scribner's, 1972), pp. 61–63; "World Missiles," *Flight International*, May 29, 1976, p. 1432; and Georg Panyalev, "Backfire—Soviet Counter to American B-1," *International Defense Review*, vol. 8 (April 1975), p. 641.

a. Shorter distance at low altitude, longer at high altitude.
b. Would require mid-course guidance for certain missions or at maximum range.
c. Two-thirds of the Bears carry the AS-3.

Table 2-8. Characteristics of Soviet Frontal Aviation, 1950–77

	Airplanes		
Year	Number	Type	Remarks
1950	16,000	MIG-9, MIG-15, LA-9, LA-11, LA-15, IL-2, IL-10, TU-2, YAK-9	Propeller aircraft left from World War II and early postwar designs; first jets
1955	9,600	MIG-15, MIG-17, MIG-19, LA-15, IL-28, YAK-17, YAK-23	Modern jets; propeller aircraft out of service; first supersonic aircraft
1960	4,000	MIG-15, MIG-17, MIG-19, MIG-21, SU-7, IL-28	First Mach 2 aircraft; air-to-air missiles introduced
1965	3,200	MIG-17, MIG-19, MIG-21, IL-28, YAK-27, YAK-28	New light bomber; aircraft equipped for use in nuclear conflict
1970	3,700	MIG-17, MIG-19, MIG-21, MIG-25, SU-7, IL-28, YAK-27, YAK-28	Increase in supersonic aircraft; drift away from pure air-superiority to multipurpose fighters; old-fashioned ordnance still in wide use
1977	4,600	MIG-17, MIG-21, MIG-23, MIG-25, MIG-27, SU-7, SU-17,SU-19, IL-28, YAK-27, YAK-28	New aircraft less agile but designed for ground attack; precision-guided air to-ground missiles

Sources: Derived from Robert A. Kilmarx, *A History of Soviet Air Power* (Praeger, 1962), p. 227; Wolfe, *Soviet Power and Europe*, p. 167; and *Allocation of Resources—1975*, Hearings, p. 148. For a complete historical order-of-battle inventory for the USSR and Warsaw Pact, see *Armed Forces Journal*, Aug. 17, 1970, p. 34.

attack. It has been the largest component of all the Soviet air forces since World War II. Its force levels declined sharply between World War II and 1960 (table 2-8),[36] but rose modestly after 1967, as hostility with China grew and military planning began to emphasize conventional warfare.[37] The current composition of Frontal Aviation is shown in table 2-9.

Although it did receive MIG-15 Fagots and IL-28 Beagles in the late 1940s and early 1950s, Frontal Aviation was not completely reequipped with first-generation jet aircraft until the early 1960s (the states of Western Europe, in particular West Germany, did not seriously build up their forces until after 1960). Clearly, strategic air defense was paramount in Soviet planning.

Until the late 1950s the Soviet Union's primary instrument for striking deep into Europe was Long Range Aviation. Frontal Aviation was ex-

36. Wolfe, *Soviet Power and Europe*, p. 167.
37. *Allocation of Resources in the Soviet Union and China—1975*, Hearings before the Subcommittee on Priorities and Economy in Government of the Joint Economic Committee, 94:1 (GPO, 1975), pt. 1, p. 148.

Table 2-9. Composition of Frontal Aviation, 1977[a]

Aircraft	Number	First year in service[b]	Purpose
MIG-17 Fresco	220	1952	Ground support
MIG-21 Fishbed D, J, K, and L	1,450	1963, 1970, 1973	Air combat, ground attack
MIG-23 Flogger B	740	1971	Air combat
MIG-27 Flogger D	360	1973	Ground attack
SU-7 Fitter	500	1959	Ground support
SU-17 Fitter C	300	1971	Ground attack
SU-19 Fencer	150	1975	Ground attack
IL-28 Beagle	45	1950	Ground attack
YAK-28 Brewer A, B, and C	115	1963	Ground attack
MI-8 Hip	150	1961	Air assault, ground support
MI-24 Hind	300	1973	Ground support, air assault
MIG-21 Fishbed H	300	1970	Reconnaissance
MIG-25 Foxbat B	115	1971	Reconnaissance
IL-28 Beagle	80	1950	Reconnaissance
YAK-27 Mangrove	170	1959	Reconnaissance
YAK-28 Brewer D and E	45	1964	Electronic warfare
AN-12 Cub C	5	c	Electronic warfare
IL-18 Crate	5	c	Electronic warfare

Sources: Derived from IISS, *The Military Balance 1977–1978*, p. 10; Raso, Tauri, and Caiti, "Le Forze Aeromissilistiche," p. 2; "Military Aircraft of the World," *Flight International*, Mar. 6, 1976; and "World's Air Forces," *Flight International*, June 26, 1976, p. 1762.

a. Does not include 2,550 helicopters used for transport and liaison duties, 1,050 training airplanes, or 250 transport planes.

b. If year introduced into service is not known, it is the year that the aircraft was first observed.

c. Unknown.

pected to provide air defense for ground forces in rear areas until large numbers of surface-to-air missiles could be brought into operation; its only offensive craft in forward areas were about 200 IL-28 Beagles deployed in Eastern Europe.[38]

When Soviet theater forces began to acquire nuclear weapons in the 1960s, Frontal Aviation units, instead of being assigned a nuclear role, were reduced further in importance as Khrushchev channeled resources into building up the missile forces. Simultaneously a new family of battlefield missiles—the Frog introduced in 1957, two Scud versions in 1957 and 1965, and the Scaleboard in 1967—was issued to Soviet army divisions and groups for use in nuclear and chemical strikes.

After a time, however, the fascination with surface-to-surface missiles as an inexpensive replacement for manned aircraft gave way to a more

38. Wolfe, *Soviet Power and Europe*, p. 40.

balanced concept.[39] Although the number of aircraft assigned to Frontal Aviation continued to drop, the new models issued—MIG-21 Fishbeds, SU-7 Fitters, and YAK-28 Brewers—performed better than the old in air combat, ground support, and ground attack, and they were improved continually. The MIG-21, for example, evolved from a day-only interceptor, to an all-weather air-superiority fighter, and finally to a multipurpose fighter.[40] Older aircraft that were not retired were converted for reconnaissance and electronic warfare or transferred to the forces of the USSR's allies. Some, though, such as the MIG-17, remained in service with Soviet air forces through the mid-1970s.

In 1968 a numerical buildup began in Frontal Aviation, and by 1976 Frontal Aviation's strength in the Far East had doubled.[41] In Europe a qualitative change became evident in the 1970s when aircraft began to appear that had been designed in the 1950s and 1960s for tactical nuclear warfare. As the possibility of a conventional war in Europe became widely accepted, a variety of demanding requirements for air operations built up. NATO airfields and formations of ground troops were added to the list of targets to be annihilated so that Soviet ground forces could advance effectively.[42] These requirements called for an air force with longer range aircraft able to carry heavier conventional combat loads and to fly at low altitudes to add shock and staying power for the offensive. To provide this versatility, MIG-21 Fishbed J, K, and Ls, MIG-23 and MIG-27 Floggers, SU-17 Fitter Cs, and SU-19 Fencers began to replace less capable aircraft (see table 2-10).[43] The third-generation aircraft entering Frontal Aviation service in the 1970s have nearly double the offensive load capacity of the second generation and are almost 70 percent more versatile.

Frontal Aviation aircraft are now being built for the modern battlefield, to take part in air-combat and ground-attack operations, and to do patrol duty that includes escorting strike forces and longer range bombers. The wheel may have turned full circle: the design for the next type of inter-

39. Ibid., pp. 205–06.
40. Green and Swanborough, *The Observer's Soviet Aircraft Directory,* pp. 170–76.
41. Secretary of Defense Donald H. Rumsfeld, "Annual Defense Department Report FY 1977" (Jan. 27, 1976; processed), p. 126.
42. Present estimates of rates of advance are 25–30 miles per day in a conventional war and double that in a nuclear war.
43. R. Meller, "Europe's New Generation of Combat Aircraft," *International Defense Review,* vol. 8 (April 1975), p. 175; "Fitter C—Link Between 2nd and 3rd Generation Soviet Attack Aircraft," *International Defense Review,* vol. 9 (April 1976), p. 167; Georg Panyalev, "The SU 19 Fencer—Threat to Western Europe," *International Defense Review,* vol. 9 (February 1976), p. 67.

Table 2-10. Capabilities of Frontal Aviation's Aircraft in Three Design Generations, 1946–75

Design generation and aircraft	Ordnance load (tons)	Maximum combat radius (miles)	Offensive load carrying capacity[a]	External ordnance stations[b]	Maximum speed (Mach number)
First (1946–55)					
IL-28 Beagle[c]	2.2	600	1,320	3.0[d]	0.80
MIG-15 Fagot	0.5	280	140	2.0	0.87
MIG-17 Fresco	0.5	360	180	2.0	0.96
MIG-19 Farmer	0.5	400	200	2.0	1.35
Average	0.9	410	460	2.3	n.a.
Second (1956–65)					
MIG-21 Fishbed D	1.0	200	200	2.0	2.00
SU-7 Fitter	2.0	300	600	6.0	2.00
YAK-28 Brewer	2.2	500	1,100	3.0[d]	1.10
Average	1.7	333	633	3.7	n.a.
Third (1966–75)					
MIG-23 Flogger B	2.2	525	1,155	5.0	2.30
MIG-27 Flogger D	2.2	600	1,320	7.0	1.60
SU-17 Fitter C	3.0	600	1,800	8.0	1.60
MIG-21 Fishbed J	1.0	400	400	5.0	2.10
SU-19 Fencer	5.0	800	4,000	6.0	2.30
Average	2.7	585	1,735	6.2	n.a.

Sources: Green and Swanborough, *The Observer's Soviet Aircraft Directory*, pp. 53, 143, 162, 170, 177, 203, 210, and 242; and R. Meller, "Europe's New Generation of Combat Aircraft," pp. 180–81.
n.a. = not applicable.
a. Maximum combat radius times ordnance load.
b. Hard points to which bombs, missiles, spare fuel tanks, or electronic parts can be attached; the number is a measure of versatility.
c. A Chinese version of the IL-28 Beagle is reported to have an ordnance load of 3.3 tons (*Allocation of Resources in the Soviet Union and China—1976*, Hearings before the Subcommittee on Priorities and Economy in Government of the Joint Economic Committee, 94:2 [GPO, 1976], p. 94).
d. Includes internal storage area for bombs.

ceptor to be delivered to PVO Strany is based on a combat fighter designed for Frontal Aviation.[44]

Around 15 percent of Frontal Aviation's inventory is being replaced each year by six types of aircraft: the multipurpose MIG-21 Fishbed J, K, and L; the MIG-23 Flogger B air-combat fighter; the MIG-27 Flogger D, SU-17 Fitter C, and SU-19 Fencer ground-attack aircraft; and the MIG-25 Foxbat B reconnaissance aircraft. About 38 percent of Frontal Aviation's aircraft are models of the MIG-21 used for fighter, ground-attack, and reconnaissance requirements; 36 percent the SU-17, SU-19, MIG-23, MIG-25, and MIG-27; and 26 percent such older types as the MIG-17,

44. A version of the MIG-23 Flogger.

SU-7, YAK-27, YAK-28, and IL-28. Frontal Aviation appears to be larger now than it has been since the 1950s; over the next five years it is likely to remain fairly stable at 4,600 airplanes.[45] The number of combat helicopters though is expected to increase rapidly.

As battle concepts have changed in recent years, support missions for tactical aircraft have become increasingly important. Tactical aircraft that can be used for reconnaissance and electronic warfare missions before and after battle make up about 16 percent of Frontal Aviation's inventory. These are mostly MIG-21 Fishbed Hs, MIG-25 Foxbat Bs, IL-28 Beagles, YAK-27 Mangroves, and YAK-28 Brewer Ds and Es. The service also has AN-12 Cub Cs and IL-18 Crates for use in electronic warfare. The MIG-25 Foxbat gives both Frontal Aviation and Soviet commanders flexibility in reconnaissance that probably makes it superior to satellite photographs (Foxbats are also designed to the PVO Strany). The altitudes and speeds at which the Foxbat performs best allow it to outdistance most modern interceptor aircraft.[46]

New developments in tactical air-to-ground weaponry have also enhanced Frontal Aviation's capabilities. Though its aircraft were able to deliver high-explosive bombs of all sizes, unguided air-to-ground rockets, antipersonnel weapons, and radar-guided air-to-ground missiles such as the AS-7 Kerry,[47] the USSR's development of air-to-ground ordnance lagged behind that of Western nations in the early 1960s. The Soviet view of conventional ordnance's marginal application on the European battlefields now seems to have changed.[48] The SU-19 Fencer and MIG-27 Flogger D have range finders that use laser energy rather than attack radar,[49] and both planes have terrain-avoidance radar and optical and antiradar sensors. They are thus capable of launching television- or laser-guided bombs and missiles that seek out the enemy's radar. In addition, work is continuing on a new generation of fuel-air explosives. Finally, air-to-air weapons that in the past were largely designed to home onto a high-flying bomber's jet exhaust, with enough range to avoid a SAC bomber's rearward-firing cannon, and to turn with relatively slow-moving aircraft

45. *Allocation of Resources—1975,* Hearings, pp. 104 and 148.

46. Green and Swanborough, *The Observer's Soviet Aircraft Directory,* p. 180.

47. Peter Bogart, "The Air Attack Potential of the Warsaw Pact," *International Defense Review,* vol. 9 (April 1976), p. 197.

48. Rumsfeld, "Annual Defense Department Report FY 1977," p. 127; see also "Air Power for the Pact," *Flight International,* June 5, 1976, p. 1522.

49. "New Russian Weapons," *Flight International,* Nov. 20, 1975, p. 752, and July 10, 1976, p. 79.

at high altitudes are being improved or replaced by weapons useful in combat with aircraft that are capable of high-energy turns.

Both its aircraft and their equipment are increasingly being built to Frontal Aviation's own specifications rather than being modifications of aircraft and ordnance designed for PVO Strany. The ability to supply both major fighter forces with capable aircraft is a luxury not known in the Soviet air forces until the early 1970s. The decisions to shift to a dual emphasis reflect the reduction in Soviet air-defense requirements as the U.S. strategic bomber force shrinks in tandem with the growth of ballistic missiles. Two fairly recent developments important to Soviet planning—emphasis on the ability to fight the conventional phase of a war in Europe, and the deployment of mobile missile launchers and radar-controlled gun-fire systems with Soviet ground divisions—have profound implications for NATO and U.S. tactical air force planning; they are discussed on pages 73–77 below.

Military Transport Aviation

Military Transport Aviation is primarily responsible for supporting the Soviet armed forces, particularly ground units, with air-lifted supplies, weapons, and personnel throughout the USSR and foreign combat areas. In support of Soviet political commitments it also delivers supplies or people, whether for relief after natural disasters or for wars, on short notice. Its role in a Soviet offensive, however, is the transport of combat troops. It is capable of moving about one airborne division over a long distance, and two to three for short distances. Military Transport aircraft are like those of Aeroflot, and thus the civilian planes can be used in instances where the armed forces do not wish to be obvious, as seems to have been the case during the Angolan civil war. Aeroflot is more important, though, as a replacement pool for pilots, and a reserve center for training.

The first Soviet aircraft designed for tactical airlift, the AN-8 Camp, first flown in 1955, was replaced in four years by the AN-12 Cub (a derivative of a commercial transport). The AN-12 became the standard combat transport in Military Transport, greatly increasing the service's lift capacity and thus the mobility of the Soviet armed forces. The AN-12 is able to carry up to twenty tons of cargo, including small armored fighting

Table 2-11. Characteristics of Helicopters in Soviet Air Forces, 1950–77[a]

Helicopter	Year first observed	Principal use	Typical load
MI-4 Hound	1951	cargo transport	1.8 tons[b]
MI-6 Hook	1957	cargo transport	16.8 tons[e]
MI-10 Harke	1961	cargo transport	25.0 tons[d]
MI-8 Hip	1961	troop transport	1/16 battalion
MI-24 Hind[a]	1971	ground attack	[e]

Sources: Green and Swanborough, *The Observer's Soviet Aircraft Directory*, p. 187; and "Military Helicopters," *Flight International*, July 17, 1976, p. 183.
  a. There are also MI-1 Hares and MI-2 Hoplites used for liaison and utility work.
  b. Including one light armored vehicle.
  c. Carries equipment too large to be carried by other helicopters.
  d. A normal battalion consists of 500 combat infantrymen.
  e. All variants (A, B, C, and D) of the Hind model can carry four 57 mm rocket pods, Swatter or AS-8 antitank weapons, and a 12.7 mm cannon or a multibarreled Gatling gun. The Hind D has improved sensors and seems more capable in attack roles than the others.

vehicles, or a hundred paratroopers. New versions began to enter the inventory in 1968. There are about six hundred in service.

For long-range military transport, the Russians depend on the AN-22 Cock; about two-thirds of their fleet of seventy-five is in operation at any one time. This aircraft can carry up to eighty tons of cargo, including different types of battlefield missiles, surface-to-air missile units, assault guns, and unassembled fighter aircraft. Introduction of the AN-22 between 1965 and 1975 increased Military Transport's capacity and made new distant regions accessible to Soviet involvement.

In the mid-1970s a third aircraft began to be added to Military Transport. The IL-76 Candid, which was first flown in 1971, is technologically like the United States' C-5 Galaxy, but in appearance, performance, and lift capacity it is more like the smaller C-141 Starlifter.[50] It is expected that the IL-76 will augment the AN-22 in transport regiments in the late 1970s and the 1980s. In addition a medium transport plane able to take off and land on short strips is reportedly under development and will probably replace some of the AN-12s.

For light transport and resupply within theaters, Military Transport Aviation relies primarily on helicopters. Over the years they have become more versatile. Frontal Aviation in addition to attack helicopters has its own helicopters for moving troops directly into action (table 2-11).[51]

  50. Green and Swanborough, *The Observer's Soviet Aircraft Directory*, pp. 151–52.
  51. Graham H. Turbiville, "A Soviet View of Heliborne Assault Operations," *Military Review*, vol. 55 (October 1975), pp. 3 and 6.

Table 2-12. Capabilities of Military Transport Aviation's Aircraft, 1965, 1970, and 1977

Aircraft	1965	1970	1977
Number	490	805	685
Aggregate lift capacity (millions of tons per mile)[a]	11.4	19.4	26.4

Sources: Green and Swanborough, *The Observer's Soviet Aircraft Directory*, pp. 36–37, 124–25, and 128–29; and IISS, *The Military Balance 1977–1978*, p. 10.

a. The product of combat range and lift capacity per day, summed over major transport types in the force.

By 1977 Military Transport Aviation was responsible for 710 airlift planes, 790 general-purpose transport and liaison aircraft, and over 320 helicopters made up of about 160 MI-1s, MI-2s, and MI-4s along with 160 MI-6s and MI-8s as well as some MI-10s and MI-24s.[52] Its capacity to move troops and cargo has increased over a third since 1970 even though its complement of aircraft has declined (table 2-12).

Eastern European Air Forces

The air forces of the Soviet Union's allies in the Warsaw Pact presently operate about 2,500 aircraft (table 2-13). Two-thirds are designed for air defense, over a fourth for ground attack, and the remainder for reconnaissance.[53] As new equipment comes in to bolster air-defense units, especially late-model MIG-21 Fishbed Ls, these forces may be able to assume other duties, such as ground attack, more readily.

In any conflict in Central Europe the countries in the northern tier would be involved more quickly and directly than those in the southern tier. Poland and Czechoslovakia have both air-defense and tactical air armies. Thus they, as well as most of the Warsaw Pact forces, would be involved in all Soviet operations and could play a significant role. Over 40 percent of the 1,700 combat aircraft of the northern tier belong to Poland. The Polish air force, because it is willing to pay for it, has high priority in

52. Green and Swanborough, *The Observer's Soviet Aircraft Directory*, pp. 181–99; and IISS, *The Military Balance 1976–1977*, p. 10.

53. IISS, *The Military Balance 1977–1978*, pp. 13–15. In 1977 East Germany assigned 85 percent of its aircraft to air defense, Czechoslovakia 53 percent, Poland 58 percent, Hungary 71 percent, Rumania 72 percent, and Bulgaria 72 percent. The balance of their aircraft were assigned to ground-attack, reconnaissance, and electronic-warfare missions.

Table 2-13. Number of Aircraft in Eastern European Air Forces, 1955–77

	Number of aircraft				
Air forces	*1955*	*1960*	*1965*	*1970*	*1977*
Northern tier	1,620	1,700	1,700	1,650	1,719
East Germany	100	200	350	300	416
Czechoslovakia	720	650	600	500	558
Poland	800	850	750	850	745
Southern tier	1,070	770	720	700	773
Hungary	350	100	150	150	176
Rumania	320	370	270	300	327
Bulgaria	400	300	300	250	270
Total	2,690	2,470	2,420	2,350	2,492

Sources: IISS, *The Military Balance 1977–1978*, pp. 13–15; and "The Soviet Union Moves Ahead: On Land, on the Sea, and in the Air," *Armed Forces Journal*, Aug. 17, 1970, pp. 34–36.

receiving new equipment. For example, it was the first Warsaw Pact country to receive the SU-20, the export version of the SU-17 Fitter C.[54] The Czech air force is evenly divided between air-defense and ground-attack aircraft and reportedly may soon receive MIG-23 Floggers to replace its early-model MIGs. The East German air force is heavily weighted toward defense, although some reports indicate it has received a version of the MI-24 Hind for tactical use.

The southern tier air forces have the least modern aircraft of all Pact nations, being akin to Soviet Frontal Aviation forces in the early and mid-1960s. They tend to place last in modernization programs, even behind recipients in the Third World.

From 1955 to 1977 the size of the Eastern European air forces decreased by about 7 percent as newer and more capable equipment entered their inventories. Northern tier air forces have increased, however, because of their increased responsibilities in a theater war. The cuts were in the southern tier forces, which lost almost one-third of their aircraft inventory as a result of the decreased threat from the U.S. Strategic Air Command and Sixth Fleet and of the revamping of the Hungarian air force after the 1956 revolt. Their equipment, like that of the Soviet air forces, has been reoriented from an emphasis on defense to an ability to perform the multiple tasks expected of a modern air army.

54. "The Warsaw Pact Air Forces," *Royal Air Force Yearbook, 1975*, pp. 46 and 47.

Organization and Deployment

Within each one of the Soviet air forces, organization and deployment depend on the functional needs of the Soviet military as a whole. Frontal Aviation, Military Transport Aviation, and the Naval Air Force work closely with higher organizational entities; both PVO Strany and Long Range Aviation, which is under air force control, are relatively independent in determining how to allocate their forces.

All five of the forces have a rigid structure that rarely permits regiments or squadrons to be shifted around. No more than a few regiments are involved in training deployments at any one time.

The largest unit of the air forces is the air army, which is made up of air divisions, each equipped with a single type of aircraft. Operations usually are conducted at the regimental and squadron level. Three regiments make a division, and three squadrons a regiment. One squadron in a regiment is mainly responsible for training, but remains ready to go into combat.

The number of aircraft assigned to a squadron varies. Typical PVO Strany, most Military Transport Aviation, and Frontal Aviation squadrons have twelve aircraft, while Long Range Aviation squadrons have nine or ten, and Naval Air Force squadrons nine to twelve; Military Transport Aviation squadrons have ten fixed-wing aircraft or twelve helicopters in units not assigned to other commands.[55] In the Soviet air forces, as in the U.S. air forces, only a portion of the total number of aircraft available is assigned to squadrons; the others serve as replacements for aircraft lost or being repaired or modified. The fraction of the force that is in operational readiness varies by aircraft type. For early models such as the MIG-17 or MIG-21, the operational readiness rate is said to have been as high as 80 percent. But as more sophisticated aircraft, such as the MIG-23 and SU-19, entered the inventory, the proportion available for assignment is reported to have declined perhaps to 70 percent. Indeed, reports indicate that the MIG-23 has a very low rate of availability because it has been prone to accident and difficult to maintain.[56] The limited maintenance possible at sea may permit only a 60 percent rate for naval aircraft. Also, the readiness rate differs from area to

55. Green and Swanborough, *The Observer's Soviet Aircraft Directory,* pp. 104, 105, and 108.
56. "Flying the Fishbed," *Flight International,* Sept. 25, 1975, p. 443.

Table 2-14. PVO Strany Deployment, 1977

	Aircraft	
Region	*Number*	*Type*
Special		
(Moscow and Baku districts)	600	SU-11, SU-15, MIG-25P, YAK-28P
Western USSR	900	SU-9, SU-11, SU-15, MIG-17, MIG-23P, TU-28P, YAK-28P
Southern USSR	200–250	SU-9, SU-11, MIG-17, MIG-19
Central USSR	250–300	SU-9, MIG-17
Eastern USSR	600	SU-9, SU-11, SU-15, MIG-17, MIG-19, MIG-25P, YAK-28P

Sources: Derived from Green and Swanborough, *The Observer's Soviet Aircraft Directory*, p. 102; Robert D. Archer, "The Soviet Fighters," *Space/Aeronautics*, July 1968, p. 65; and John Erickson, *Soviet–Warsaw Pact Force Levels*, USSI Report 76-2 (United States Strategic Institute, 1976), p. 45.

area; those aircraft deployed closest to combat zones—say, in East Germany—may have more spare parts on hand than those in the USSR.

The PVO Strany deploys forces in two clearly defined air-defense districts—Moscow and Baku—that are under its direct control (table 2-14). More than a fourth of the PVO's interceptors, and usually its newest aircraft, are based there. Command arrangements for the eight other air-defense districts are not evident.[57] More than a third of the PVO forces are found in western regions of the USSR. They typically receive new equipment right after the Moscow and Baku districts. They are equipped to defend high-value targets against bombers or for a NATO-Warsaw Pact war in which Western air forces might attempt deep interdiction missions against facilities in the USSR. Soviet air-defense aircraft might also be sent to assist Eastern European air defenses. Districts in the north seem to have the majority of long-range interceptors, which patrol areas beyond the range of Soviet surface-to-air missiles. These interceptors would be the first units to engage enemy bombers. In the Far East, PVO units could be used for air-combat missions, once the danger from Chinese short- and medium-range bombers was removed. PVO Strany units in the southern region were reduced sharply after 1964, as the number of U.S. bombers deployed in southern Europe and in North Africa declined and nuclear attack on the Soviet Union was removed from the missions of Sixth Fleet carriers.

57. John Erickson, "Some Developments in Soviet Tactical Aviation," *Journal of the Royal United Services Institute for Defense Studies*, vol. 120 (September 1975), p. 73.

In Eastern Europe, air forces of both the northern and southern tier nations are integrated with PVO, and make up six additional air-defense districts under the control of the Warsaw Pact commander—always a Soviet marshal.[58] As in the USSR itself, heavy antiaircraft artillery units, surface-to-air missile units, and air-defense air forces are coordinated in a plan for defending both the general area and specific targets. As currently constituted, PVO units of the Eastern European air forces could contribute some 1,500 aircraft, 124 SA-2 and 32 SA-3 missile battalions, and numerous antiaircraft artillery pieces; they would constitute the first defensive buffer for the Soviet Union.[59] In addition, there are Soviet-operated SA-3 units deployed around major Soviet air bases in Eastern Europe.

Approximately half of Frontal Aviation's 4,600 fixed-wing aircraft are positioned for the European theater; a fourth are in the Far East and the remainder serve as a ready reserve.[60] Frontal Aviation forces are organized into about fifteen air armies[61] and follow the deployment pattern of Soviet ground forces quite closely. One air army is attached to each of the groups of Soviet forces in East Germany, Poland, and Hungary. There is also a detachment of aircraft, possibly an air army, with the Central Group of Forces in Czechoslovakia. Six air armies are located in the western part of the Soviet Union and five in the southern and eastern portions.[62] Frontal Aviation falls under the purview of the local military district or group of forces commander, who is then responsible directly to the military high command.

An air army can be as large as the spearhead 16th Air Army in East Germany, with almost a thousand aircraft, or as small as the 17th Air Army in the Kiev military district, with a hundred.[63] A large air army, such as the one in East Germany, usually consists of fighter divisions, fighter-bomber divisions, reconnaissance regiments, transport regiments from Military Transport Aviation, and helicopter and support regiments. The air army in East Germany is clearly the most potent and modern one with the best trained pilots, yet there seem to be no clear priorities regarding which units first receive new equipment; a new type of aircraft could show up in any number of places before it arrived in Eastern Europe.

58. Ibid.
59. IISS, *The Military Balance 1976–1977*, pp. 12–14.
60. Moorer, "U.S. Military Posture for FY 1974," p. 52.
61. Brown, "U.S. Military Posture for FY 1977," p. 65.
62. Meller, "Europe's New Generation of Combat Aircraft," p. 178.
63. *New York Times*, Apr. 18, 1976.

Table 2-15. Frontal Aviation Deployment, 1977

	Aircraft[a]	
Military district and air army	*Number*	*Type*
Eastern Europe		
Germany: Group of Soviet Forces (16th Air Army)	975	MIG-21, MIG-23, MIG-25, MIG-27, SU-7, SU-17, MI-24, MIG-21R, YAK-28, IL-18
Poland: Northern Group of Forces (37th Air Army)	300	MIG-21, MIG-23, MIG-25, MIG-27, SU-7, SU-17, MIG-21R
Czechoslovakia: Central Group of Forces	100	MIG-21, MIG-23, MIG-27, MIG-21R
Hungary: Southern Group of Forces	250	SU-7, MIG-21, MIG-23, MIG-27, SU-7, IL-28
Northern and western USSR		
Leningrad: 13th Air Army	300	MIG-21, MIG-23, MIG-27, SU-17, MIG-21R, AN-12E
Baltic: 30th Air Army	300	MIG-21, MIG-23, MIG-27, SU-7, SU-17, SU-19, YAK-27, YAK-28, MI-24
Belorussian: 1st Air Army	300	MIG-17, MIG-21, MIG-23, MIG-27, SU-7, YAK-27, YAK-28, MI-24
Carpathian: 57th Air Army	350	MIG-17, MIG-21, MIG-23, MIG-27, SU-7, SU-19, MIG-21R, MI-24
Southern and central USSR		
Moscow: Air Reserve	125	MIG-17, MIG-21
Kiev: 17th Air Army	100	MIG-23, SU-7, IL-28, MI-8
Odessa: 5th Air Army	250	MIG-23, MIG-27, YAK-27, MI-8
Trans Caucasus: 34th Air Army	300	MIG-21, MIG-23, MIG-27, YAK-27, MI-24
Turkestan: 6th Air Army	175	MIG-21, MIG-23, MIG-21R, MI-8
Far Eastern USSR		
Central Asian, Siberian, Trans Baikal, and Far Eastern districts: Far Eastern Air Forces	1,225	MIG-17, MIG-21, MIG-23, MIG-27, MIG-21R, MIG-25R, SU-7, SU-17, SU-19, MI-8, MI-24, IL-28, YAK-28

Sources: Derived from Meller, "Europe's New Generation of Combat Aircraft," pp. 175–80; and *Aviation Week and Space Technology*, Sept. 29, 1975, p. 57.

a. Fixed-wing planes and combat helicopters.

In time of war, air and ground armies would combine to form a front. The groups of forces in Eastern Europe are the foundation for tactical fronts; air armies not stationed abroad would combine with ground armies in their military districts.

Current deployments of Frontal Aviation (table 2-15) in Eastern Europe illustrate the Warsaw Pact nations' preoccupation with dispersal as a means of ensuring survival. In East Germany, Poland, and Czechoslovakia the Pact maintains some 170 airfields of all sizes, of which 30 are main operating bases of Soviet Frontal Aviation.[64] (In a comparable area, NATO maintains roughly one-third as many fields.) As further insurance there are several hundred grass strips that aircraft could move to in a crisis; air operations would not be long sustained from grass strips, however, because of the damage done by each sortie and because of the lack of maintenance and logistic facilities. This debility would be significant in a conventional war.

The vulnerability of its aircraft in a conventional war was sufficient to cause the USSR to begin a sheltering program in 1966. Now the main operating bases in Eastern Europe and the western USSR have fortified shelters for aircraft as well as underground maintenance and aircraft storage facilities. The success of the Israeli strike against Arab aircraft at the onset of the 1967 war, as compared to Israel's relative ineffectiveness against sheltered Arab aircraft in 1973, seems to have validated the wisdom of this construction program.[65] Interestingly enough, the PVO has begun a sheltering program to increase its aircrafts' ability to survive even in the initial stages of a nuclear missile exchange, so that they can defend against bombers.

At present, Military Transport Aviation units equipped with AN-12 Cubs for moving material and personnel are based with Frontal Aviation armies; they rotate among districts and groups. Two independent Military Transport divisions equipped with AN-22s and IL-76s are responsible for long-range airlift.[66] In 1976, 80 percent of the personnel assigned to the Group of Soviet Forces in Germany were rotated by air, reflecting a practice that has grown steadily over the years.[67]

The Soviet Naval Air Force is deployed along with the four Soviet fleets in the Northern, Baltic, Black Sea, and Pacific fleet districts (table

64. John Erickson, "MBFR: Force Levels and Security Requirements," *Strategic Review,* vol. 1 (Summer 1973), p. 34.

65. "Statement of Secretary of Defense Laird, FY 1971," p. 123. In 1967 when the Israeli air force struck Arab air bases, they destroyed 373 aircraft that were unsheltered and exposed. In 1973, when the aircraft were sheltered and dispersed, only 22 were knocked out. Of course, the element of surprise was not present in 1973. With a new generation of weapons for tactical aircraft, by the 1980s the protection offered against high-explosive bombs may be negligible.

66. "The Soviet Air Forces—An Offensive Posture and Expanding Capability," *Air International,* June 1976, p. 281.

67. John Erickson, "Soviet Military Capabilities in Europe," *Journal of the Royal United Services Institute for Defense Studies,* vol. 120 (March 1975), pp. 65–69.

Table 2-16. Naval Air Force Deployment, 1977

		Number			
			Fleet		
Aircraft	*Total*	*Northern*	*Baltic*	*Black Sea*	*Pacific*
Land-based					
TU-16 Badger B, C, G	280	85	50	60	85
TU-22 Blinder C	48	. . .	10	20–25	15
Backfire B	35	10	10	15	. . .
SU-17 Fitter C	40	. . .	40	. . .	. . .
YAK-36 Forger	20	. . .	. . .	20	. . .
TU-16 Badger D, E, F	149	45	30	30	40–45
TU-20 Bear D, F	60ª	40	. . .	. . .	20
BE-12 Mail	90	30	10	40	10
IL-38 May	55	30	. . .	10	15
MI-4 Hound, MI-14 Haze, KA-25 Hormone A, MI-8 Hip	185–190	b	b	b	b
Miscellaneousᶜ	153	b	b	b	b
Total land-based	1,115–1,120	310–315	255	215	335
*Ship-based*ᵈ					
YAK-36 Forger	10	10	. . .	. . .	. . .
KA-25 Hormone A, B	70–75	25	5	37	6
Total ship-based	80–85	35	5	37	6
Total	1,200	350	260	250	340

Sources: Derived from "United States Military Posture for FY 1974, by Chairman of the Joint Chiefs of Staff, Admiral Thomas H. Moorer, USN" (Mar. 26, 1973; processed), p. 53; *Air International*, October 1976, p. 155; and Jean Laboyle Coubat, "Combat Fleets of the World 1976/1977," *Aviation Week and Space Technology*, Jan. 24, 1977, p. 44.

a. About 15 are Bear Fs, also referred to by design bureau designation as TU-142s.
b. Number varies widely.
c. Includes AN-12 Cub Cs.
d. Number for which deck space is available.

2-16). About one-half of the total aircraft are assigned to the Northern and Baltic fleet areas. The Black Sea Fleet, which supports operations in the Mediterranean, has better year-round training facilities than Russia's other European fleets have. It thus receives new equipment like the Backfire bomber sooner than the others.[68] It also has the largest proportion of ship-based aircraft. The Pacific Fleet accounts for nearly 30 percent of naval aviation forces. Interestingly, there is a good deal of movement of aircraft within fleets; and within theaters such as Europe, planes may not be wedded to their home fleet areas.

68. "Backfire Aloft," *Newsweek*, Mar. 15, 1976, p. 19.

Table 2-17. Long Range Aviation Deployment, 1977

	Number oriented toward			
Aircraft	*Western Europe*	*China*	*Ocean areas and North America*	*Total*
TU-16 Badger A	203	102	0	305
TU-16 Badger[a]	83	42	0	125
TU-20 Bear A, B, C, E	0	0	104	104
TU-22 Blinder[b]	98	48	0	146
Backfire B	25	10	0	35
MYA-4 Bison A	0	0	35	35
MYA-4 Bison tanker	0	0	44	44
Total	409	202	183	794

Source: IISS, *The Military Balance 1976–1977*, p. 8.
a. Tanker reconnaissance, and electronic warfare versions.
b. All versions.

Long Range Aviation is organized into three air armies.[69] Two are located in the western Soviet Union, distributed among various military districts. The third, equipped mostly with TU-16s and TU-22s, is deployed in the Far East. The deployment of Long Range Aviation (table 2-17) is flexible enough to allow its aircraft to move to bases convenient to naval operations if their help is needed.

69. John Erickson, "Soviet Military Power," *Strategic Review*, vol. 1 (Spring 1973), p. 62.

CHAPTER THREE

SOVIET AIRCRAFT DESIGN

One of the better indicators of the type of war the Soviet Union is preparing to fight is the state of its air forces. Aviation, primarily because of the high rate at which equipment is replaced, its technological sophistication, and its distinctive characteristics, provides strong evidence of trends in combat strength. The trends in aircraft design do not necessarily correspond to the tenure of political regimes, but are governed by advances in technology and the nature of the threat posed by potential enemies. They provide one way of understanding trends in doctrine and in development of weapons and equipment for the Soviet military as a whole.

Clearly, the Soviet Union is now emphasizing development of ground-attack and multipurpose aircraft. Monthly production, at about thirty factories, of these types of aircraft has been growing and that of air-defense models decreasing slightly (table 3-1). Both new aircraft and improved versions of earlier designs are currently being produced. The MIG-21 Fishbed J, K, and L now being built are like the earlier MIG-21s in name only. They are notably more capable in air combat, can carry heavier bomb loads to attack ground targets, and carry electronic equipment for jamming enemy radar. The SU-17 Fitter C is a dramatic example of what can be accomplished through modification; it has shifted from a fixed-wing to a swing-wing aircraft, able to fly much greater distances and carry much heavier loads in combat. The MIG-23 Flogger was initially a fighter, but the MIG-27 modification is a ground-attack plane similar in certain respects to the British-French Jaguar; nearly one-third of the Floggers now being produced are ground-attack planes.

The most recent aircraft, the SU-19 Fencer, is unique in that it has a second crew member—a weapon system officer—and is assigned to

Table 3-1. Soviet Aircraft Production Rates, 1976

Design bureau and type	Number built per month	Change since 1975
Mikoyan		
MIG-21 Fishbed H, J, K, and L	15–25[a]	none
MIG-23 and MIG-27 Flogger B, C, D, E, and F	25–35[a]	increase
MIG-25 Foxbat A, B, C, and D	5	none
Sukhoi		
SU-15 Flagon E and F	5	none
SU-17 Fitter C	15[a]	increase
SU-19 Fencer	5	increase
Tupolev		
Backfire B	2–3	increase
Yakolev		
YAK-36 Forger	1–2	none
Ilyushin		
IL-76 Candid	1–2[b]	none
Mil		
MI-8 Hip	40–60	decrease
MI-24 Hind	10–15	increase

Sources: Derived from "The Growing Threat—New Soviet Weapons Technology," *Aviation Week and Space Technology*, Oct. 4, 1971, p. 9; "The Soviet Air Forces," *Air International*, June 1976, p. 277; *Newsweek*, Oct. 8, 1973, and Mar. 15, 1976; *New York Times*, Dec. 26, 1975, and Oct. 10, 1973; di Carlo Raso, Alf a Tauri, and Pierangelo Caiti, "Le Forze Aeromissilistiche dell'Est," *Aerei*, vol. 4, no. 6 (June 1976), pp. 18–20; and Herbert J. Coleman, "Soviets Push Huge Arms Buildup," *Aviation Week and Space Technology*, Apr. 12, 1976, p. 13.
a. Including exports.
b. Not including aircraft built for Aeroflot.

Frontal Aviation units.[1] Another different design is a helicopter gunship, the MI-24 Hind, which is to be one of Frontal Aviation's primary ground-support aircraft.[2] The new aircraft and the modifications of older planes mark a drift away from the emphasis on pure fighters.

In the air-defense force, SU-15 Flagons, which were produced at a rate of fifteen per month in 1971, have been replaced in production by the Flagon E and F, with added cannons, new wings, and greater maneuverability at low altitudes.[3]

1. Georg Panyalev, "The SU 19 Fencer—Threat to Western Europe," *International Defense Review*, vol. 9 (February 1976), p. 67.
2. Alexander Malzeyev, "The Soviet Mi 24-*Hind* Combat Helicopter," *International Defense Review*, vol. 8 (June 1975), p. 879. There are also reports of a smaller attack helicopter that may complement the Hind in ground-support operations; up to 50 may already be in testing.
3. "The Growing Threat—New Soviet Weapons Technology," *Avitaion Week and Space Technology*, Oct. 4, 1971, p. 9.

Maneuverability

Among the many measures and formulas for describing how well an aircraft can maneuver through the air is wing loading, the ratio of the weight of the aircraft to the area of the wing. The lower the number, the greater the ability of the plane to turn quickly at a given speed and altitude. Consequently, the lower the number, the more capable is the aircraft of surviving in air combat. The wing-loading factors for successive Soviet planes are shown in figure 3-1.

With advances in wing shape and structure, wing technology has also become an important measure of maneuverability. Wing design has so improved the turning ability of U.S. combat aircraft such as the F-15, F-16, and A-10 that they are much more agile than even their relatively low wing-loading factors would indicate. Another advance that gives a plane optimum maneuverability in a turn is the swing wing, whose shape can be changed in flight. The extra weight of the wings is their major drawback.

With the exception of swing wings, the Soviet Union has not displayed the kind of technological advances the West has made using composite materials and new wing configurations. Consequently, the 118 percent increase in the wing-loading factor of Mikoyan-designed aircraft and a 30 percent increase in Sukhoi designs since 1948 may be significant. A particularly notable rise took place in the mid-1960s, as the third generation of tactical aircraft began to appear.

With one exception, Mikoyan designs in recent years have tried to improve the agility of aircraft despite their greater payloads and ranges by adopting swing wings and holding weight increases to a minimum. Nonetheless, much of the maneuverability that made the early MIGs good for air combat has disappeared with the addition of heavy avionic equipment, hard points on the wings for carrying weapons, and larger storage areas for fuel. A MIG-23 Flogger B has better avionics, more speed, a higher ceiling, and more thrust than the earlier MIG-15, but at some altitudes the MIG-15 might still have a defensive advantage. The MIG-25 Foxbat, the aircraft with the highest wing-loading factor, was built as a high-altitude interceptor and thus emphasized top speed (over Mach 3.0) at the expense of maneuverability at low altitudes.

Sukhoi products have always had higher wing-loading factors than contemporary Mikoyan products. They are designed to carry the large

Figure 3-1. Wing Loading of Selected Soviet Fighters

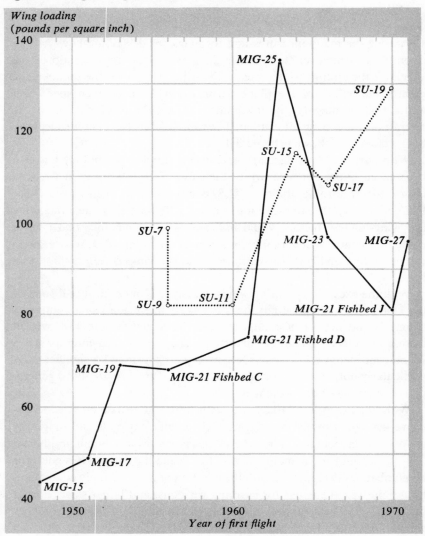

*Wing loading
(pounds per square inch)*

Sources: Derived from R. Meller, "Europe's New Generation of Combat Aircraft," *International Defense Review*, vol. 8 (April 1975), pp. 180–81, 534, and 544–45; William Green, *The World Guide to Combat Planes* (Doubleday, 1967), vol. 1, pp. 110, 115, 126, 130, 133, 140, 143, 150, 158, and 161; and William Green and Dennis Punnett, *MacDonald World Air Power Guide* (Doubleday, 1963), pp. 28–30.

loads of conventional weapons needed in ground attacks. To make room for weapons and more fuel, their airframes have been strengthened and made much heavier. Their wing areas though have also been increased.[4] Still they are less maneuverable aircraft.

Engine Performance

An aircraft's ability to accelerate and climb and to sustain a turn is another indicator of its worthiness in air combat. This ability increases as the ratio of its engine's thrust to the aircraft's weight increases. Since 1948, thrust-to-weight ratios in Mikoyan designs have gone up by 77 percent while those in Sukhoi designs have only increased by 12 percent (figure 3-2).

Increases in thrust were a way to keep performance high as aircraft grew heavier and could fly faster. The fastest accelerators—the SU-15 and MIG-23 in PVO Strany and the MIG-23 in Frontal Aviation—which form the backbone of the Soviet fighter force, have sufficient energy to be competitive in air combat. The MIG-21 is an example of how a proven light design could be steadily increased in weight, and thus ability to carry weapons, and simultaneously improved in engine performance, the end result being a 15–20 percent greater thrust-to-weight ratio.

The payoff for heavier aircraft with high wing-loading factors and modest thrust-to-weight ratios is the increase in weapons they can carry or distances they can fly. For those advantages, particularly with the SU-19 Fencer (figure 3-3), they sacrifice agility at certain performance regimes.

Design Options

Modern aircraft fall into four general categories: air-superiority fighters, requiring a high thrust-to-weight ratio and a low wing-loading

4. Another good example of how the demand for greater range has been met is the position of the air inlets for the engine. First- and second-generation aircraft such as the MIG-17 in 1952 and the SU-7, SU-9, and MIG-21 in 1956 had one central engine inlet that simplified maintenance but limited the places to house fuel. Beginning with third-generation aircraft such as the MIG-23 and SU-15 in the mid-sixties, air inlets were moved to the side, allowing increased space for fuel in the plane's body and thus greater range.

Figure 3-2. Acceleration and Climb of Selected Soviet Fighters

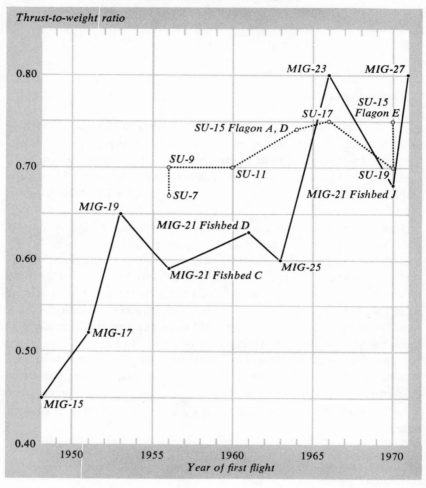

factor; interceptors, for which both thrust-to-weight ratio and wing-loading factor are generally in the medium range and emphasis is placed on top speed; ground-attack aircraft, which have a medium thrust-to-weight ratio and a high wing-loading factor, thus permitting heavy bomb loads and long range; and close-air-support aircraft, which have low-power engines and thus a medium thrust-to-weight ratio to allow them to loiter over a battlefield, and either a low wing-loading factor or well-

Figure 3-3. Ordnance and Range of Selected Soviet Fighters

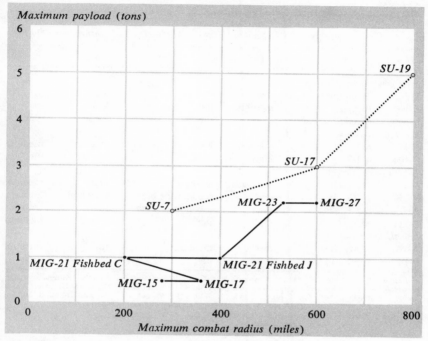

Sources: Same as figure 3-1.

designed wings to give them reasonable agility if confronted by enemy aircraft. The performance factors of various Soviet aircraft are compared to those of U.S. aircraft in table 3-2.

In the mid-1950s and early 1960s U.S. planes had medium or high wing-loading factors and modest thrust-to-weight ratios and were thus most suitable for interdiction and low-level nuclear strikes. Currently the emphasis in U.S. design is shifting to high-thrust, low wing-loading, multipurpose planes suitable for air combat. On the other hand, Soviet aircraft began in the 1950s with low wing-loading factors and medium thrust-to-weight ratios and were most useful for interception and defense of specific targets. Newer Soviet aircraft, however, display higher wing-loading factors and relatively more modest thrust-to-weight ratios, reflecting an emphasis on multipurpose and ground-attack planes.

When development of third-generation aircraft has been completed, Soviet air-defense and tactical forces will be at a threshold. Continuation of current trends into the fourth-generation jets would permit the air-

Table 3-2. Performance Characteristics of Selected U.S. and Soviet Tactical Aircraft

Similar aircraft		Value of wing-loading factor		Value of thrust-to-weight ratio	
U.S.	*Soviet*	*U.S.*	*Soviet*	*U.S.*	*Soviet*
First generation					
F-86	MIG-15	low	low	medium	medium
F-100	MIG-17	medium	low	low	medium
F-105	MIG-19	high	low	medium	medium
Second generation					
F-4	MIG-21	medium	low	medium	medium
F-104	SU-7	high	high	medium	medium
Third generation					
F-4E	MIG-21	medium	medium	high	medium
F-15	MIG-23[a]	low	medium or high[b]	very high	high
A-7	SU-17[a]	high	medium or high[b]	low	high
F-111[a]	SU-19[a]	high	high	medium	medium
Fourth generation					
A-10	SU G[c]	medium	medium	low	medium
F-16	MIG F[d]	low	low	very high	high

Sources: Derived from R. Meller, "Europe's New Generation of Combat Aircraft," *International Defense Review*, vol. 8 (April 1975), pp. 180–81, 534, and 544–45; William Green, *The World Guide to Combat Planes* (Doubleday, 1967), vol. 1, pp. 110, 115, 126, 130, 133, 140, 143, 150, 158, and 161; and William Green and Dennis Punnett, *MacDonald World Air Power Guide* (Doubleday, 1963), pp. 28–30.
   a. Swing wings.
   b. Value depends on wing configuration.
   c. Assumes a ground-attack aircraft.
   d. Assumes an air-combat fighter.

defense forces to acquire standoff missile aircraft with little ability to maneuver at low altitudes; they would be dependent on the quality of Soviet air-to-air missiles, which has been low. Frontal Aviation would acquire planes that could carry large payloads but could barely compete in air combat. Needless to say, it is unlikely that the patterns that have evolved since 1949 will continue across the board, for eventually Soviet aircraft would be unsuited for interception or air combat or as multipurpose planes. Thus there is likely to be continued branching, with one design bureau possibly emphasizing attack aircraft (such as the American A-7 or A-10) while others could concentrate on air-combat planes (such as the American F-15) and multipurpose aircraft that could back up both of the others.

Changes, then, are likely to occur in the development of interceptors, fighters, and bombers. Designs for planes used for air defense are likely in the immediate future to be based on present air-combat fighter designs, such as the MIG 23, whose performance characteristics are more pertinent to interception than air-combat needs. It is also probable that there will be an entirely new high-performance interceptor with a new radar in the 1980s. Aircraft optimized for air combat, like the MIG-23 or a follow-on, will be able to react in a wider variety of circumstances than are aircraft such as the MIG-25, which are only expected to perform properly at high speeds and at altitudes where air friction is slight. An improved radar and other modifications on the MIG-25 may keep that type of aircraft or something similar in production for a while longer. If an interim aircraft is required—for use as a long-range high-altitude air-to-air missile carrier to counter standoff bombers—then present larger aircraft such as the Fencer could be adapted. In the long run, however, a new type of aircraft to counter cruise missile carriers could be developed.

In the all-important area of air combat, aircraft in the next generation are likely to have much lower wing-loading ratios than Soviet aircraft have had since the MIG-19. Future Soviet fighters are also likely to have a better than one-to-one ratio of thrust to weight.[5] An air-combat fighter with such a strong thrust would be able to take off and land on a short runway. It might also have a double tail such as the MIG-25 Foxbat. In contrast, though, it would be both smaller and lighter, making it more survivable than current Soviet fighters.

Also, attack aircraft might be given a somewhat larger payload or greater loiter capacity. Follow-on designs to the SU-19 (whether a Sukhoi or another design product) might attempt to compensate for the concomitant loss in agility by improving the design of the wing or raising the acceleration rate. The resulting aircraft would be more useful for general air support for Soviet ground forces than for independent air operations. If a new heavy bomber is developed, it could be as a result of the work done by the Sukhoi bureau or a development by Tupolev of the Backfire. The past erratic development of bombers suggests that another design group might make a one-time effort at developing a prototype such as the Bounder in the 1950s.

Planes able to take off vertically will undoubtedly be seen at sea, where the Russians have a requirement for tactical aircraft with a vertical lift capacity. Such aircraft based on land could be widely scattered, which would increase their chances of survival. But their offensive range would be limited and logistics and maintenance problems, particularly where they are centralized as in Frontal Aviation, would be complicated. Still,

5. There have already been sporadic reports of a future air-combat fighter. The Fearless, said to have a thrust-to-weight ratio of 1.2:1 and to be similar to the F-15, turned out to be a "paper" airplane for comparing F-14 and F-15 capabilities. There are also reports of an aircraft designated MIG-29.

Table 3-3. Distribution of Types of Aircraft in Soviet and U.S. Tactical Air Forces, 1977

	Percentage of force, by aircraft			
Air force	Interceptor	Multipurpose	Attack	Reconnaissance
Soviet Frontal Aviation[a]	11	37	34	17
U.S. Air Forces in Europe	12	52	24	12

Sources: Table 2-9, above; and *Fiscal Year 1977 Authorization for Military Procurement, Research and Development, and Active Duty, Selected Reserve and Civilian Personnel Strengths*, pt. 9, *Tactical Air Power*, Hearings before the Senate Armed Services Committee, 94:2 (GPO, 1976), pp. 4860–65. Percentages may not add to 100 because of rounding.
a. Forces in Central Europe.

there are reports that some of the next generation of ground-attack aircraft might be capable of vertical takeoff. If so, the emphasis would seem to be evolving to a force that could be dispersed.

Soviet and Western Air Forces in Central Europe

The dramatic changes in Soviet aircraft design have had their strongest effect on the Soviet Frontal Aviation forces, giving them more flexibility in many areas. Frontal Aviation has proportionately more attack and reconnaissance aircraft and less multipurpose planes than the U.S. Air Force in Europe has (table 3-3).

Already the ground-attack capability of the Soviet air forces has begun to come closer to that of Western forces. Between 1965 and 1985, West Germany, the United States, and the Soviet Union each will have developed at least two generations of aircraft. Soviet Frontal Aviation in Central Europe, which had an offensive-load capacity about 34 percent as great as that of the U.S. Air Force in Europe in 1965, and 28 percent in 1975, is expected to have about 41 percent of the U.S. capacity by 1985 (figure 3-4). Its capacity was 82 percent greater than the West German Luftwaffe's in 1965, and 110 percent greater in 1975; that margin will decrease to only 19 percent in 1985 as European modernization programs come to fruition.

The groups of Soviet air forces in East Germany, Poland, Hungary, and Czechoslovakia have already experienced a 90 percent increase in their offensive load capacity since 1965: the first major increases took place with the deployment of new air detachments to Czechoslovakia in 1968 and in the early 1970s the deployment of late-model MIG-21 Fishbeds

Figure 3-4. Offensive Load Capacity of Selected European-based Air Forces, 1965, 1975, and 1985

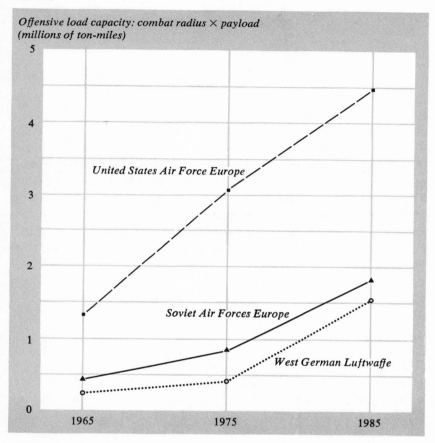

Offensive load capacity: combat radius × payload (millions of ton-miles)

and the introduction of MIG-23 and -27 Floggers in the 16th Air Army in Germany and the 37th Air Army in Poland. By 1985 there is likely to be about a 114 percent increase in offensive capability as the result of the introduction of the SU-19 Fencer in some units and fourth-generation aircraft in others. Whether this will be an accurate measure of the Russians' ability to hit their targets, however, will depend on whether they have the kind of "smart" weapons and special-area weapons the U.S. air force has recently developed, or the scatter weapons that both the U.S. and European air forces have developed, rather than the free-fall bombs and rockets the Soviet air forces now rely on.

CHAPTER FOUR

THE AIR FORCES IN ACTION

The normal peacetime activities of the Soviet air forces and the special operations that have been undertaken in support of Soviet foreign policy are guides to their potential use in wartime. For Western military planners the military support that has been given in political crises around the world suggests how Soviet forces would operate. This chapter assesses the implications of developments in Soviet air power for U.S. defense planning.

Peacetime Activity

Like most components of the Soviet armed forces, the Soviet air forces seem less concerned about their readiness to fight than do Western air forces. Planes of Frontal Aviation, for example, might be able to make, say, three sorties per day at the beginning of a war, but would drop below that level after the first five days. Western air forces' planes, by contrast, would start at about one sortie per day and stay near that level indefinitely; indeed, they could briefly move even higher at almost any point in a conflict.

The amount of flying time that can be expected of an aircraft on any given day can be gauged by the number of air crew, weapon handlers, and maintenance and administrative personnel assigned to support the air force.[1] For instance, the Luftwaffe with some 250 people per combat aircraft and the U.S. Air Forces in Europe with about 116 people per combat aircraft seem to be better prepared to use their aircraft over a

---

1. Neville Brown, *European Security 1972–1980* (London: Royal United Services Institute for Defense Studies, 1972), p. 74.

Table 4-1. Combat Aircraft per Maneuver Battalion in Soviet and U.S. Armed Forces, 1977

	Number of aircraft	
Armed forces of	*Fixed-wing planes*	*Helicopters*
Soviet Union		
Total	1.3[a]	0.2[a]
In East Germany	1.9	0.3
United States		
Total	6.4[b]	2.0[b]
In Europe	8.1	2.0

Sources: Henry Owen and Charles L. Schultze, eds., *Setting National Priorities: The Next Ten Years* (Brookings Institution, 1976), p. 98; *Fiscal Year 1977 Authorization for Military Procurement, Research and Development, and Active Duty, Selected Reserve and Civilian Personnel Strengths*, pt. 9, *Tactical Air Power*, Hearings before the Senate Armed Services Committee, 94:2 (GPO, 1976), p. 4859; *Allocation of Resources in the Soviet Union and China—1976*, Hearings before the Subcommittee on Priorities and Economy in Government of the Joint Economic Committee, 94:2 (GPO, 1976), p. 87; and Department of the Army, *Understanding Soviet Military Developments* (Department of the Army, 1977), pp. 20 and 21.

a. Assumes full mobilization.

b. Fiscal year 1978; includes air national guard and reserves.

long period of time than is the Soviet Union's 16th Air Army in East Germany, with only 67 people per combat plane.

The reason for this sharp difference in the level of support probably lies in the Western nations' greater reliance on their air forces in wartime, particularly for close air support, and the Russians' limited use of their aircraft in peacetime. The ratio of tactical aircraft to ground combat battalions is significantly lower for Soviet Frontal Aviation than it is for U.S. forces (table 4-1). This reflects both the greater number of ground units in the Soviet army and the Soviet emphasis on ground-based firepower in the initial phase of a conflict, leaving Frontal Aviation to carry out independent missions.

In peacetime the Soviet air force operates its aircraft with less frequency than does NATO. Whereas training squadrons are not associated with combat units for NATO pilots, one-third of each regiment in Frontal Aviation may be dedicated to training. NATO pilots must fly twenty hours each month; Soviet pilots may reach this level in summer months but fly as little as five hours in other months. Annually, Soviet pilots spend only about 60 percent as much time in training as U.S. pilots, though their training is more intensive.[2] Some Frontal Aviation units fly only on alternate days, others every third day, and the air force holds training exercises only infrequently. The Soviet emphasis on centraliza-

2. "Air Power for the Pact," *Flight International*, June 5, 1976, p. 1513.

tion is probably partly responsible for this inconsistency. Because all Warsaw Pact forces use the same aircraft systems, all major maintenance is carried out at central depots rather than at home bases. The cost of such a procedure in time lost meant that the average Warsaw Pact aircraft in the early 1970s spent 80 percent more time out of use per flying hour than did the average NATO aircraft.[3] While there may be budgetary advantages in this maintenance method, it plays havoc with tactical air flexibility and the rate of utilization of aircraft. Moreover, the approach is economical only for simple aircraft. It could prove even more disruptive as more advanced aircraft enter the inventory.

Air Power as a Political Instrument

Since World War II, Soviet leaders have turned often to air power to help attain both military and foreign-policy goals. In the late 1940s and early 1950s during the dispute over the status of Austria, Yugoslavia, Czechoslovakia, and West Berlin, Soviet fighter aircraft were used to harass and sometimes to shoot down U.S. and allied aircraft.[4] Western planes reconnoitering over disputed border areas in both Europe and Asia have also been victims of political battles: U.S. planes were shot down over the Baltic in 1951 and 1952; an RB-47 was harassed sixty-six miles from the Soviet border in 1958,[5] and another shot down over the Arctic in 1960;[6] in 1964 an RB-66 was intercepted and shot down when it strayed into East Germany, as was a T-39 utility plane. In the Pacific, a B-29 was brought down in 1952 in the vicinity of the Kurile Islands, and in 1953 an RB-50 was shot down over the Sea of Japan;[7] in 1954 a P-2 Neptune and an RB-29 were shot down by Soviet fighters in the vicinity of the Korean peninsula.[8] By all accounts over forty aircraft were shot down from the late 1940s through the 1960s. The Soviet air forces were used to enforce Soviet territorial or political claims and to make clear to the West the risks it would run in attempting to challenge them.

3. *Review of a Systems Analysis Evaluation of NATO vs. Warsaw Pact Conventional Forces,* Rept. of the Special Subcommittee on National Defense Posture of the House Armed Services Committee, 90:2 (GPO, 1968), p. 14.

4. See *New York Times,* Apr. 23 and 25 and May 1, 1946; Apr. 2 and 6 and July 16, 1948; Dec. 3, 1951; June 7, 1952; May 21 and 25 and Sept. 17, 1960.

5. Ibid., June 17, 1952, and Nov. 18, 1958.

6. Ibid., July 12, 1960.

7. Ibid., July 31, 1953.

8. Ibid., Sept. 6 and Nov. 8, 1954.

The Soviet Union has also been active in reconnaissance; its planes were spotted over West Germany and Denmark in 1948, the Danish Islands in 1952, Norway, Sweden, and Finland in 1954, Iran in 1959, Alaska and Canada in 1963, and Germany and Sweden in 1964.[9] The planes that flew over Alaska and Canada were from Long Range Aviation and all the others from Frontal Aviation. The flights over Alaska were staged in response to the accidental firing by U.S. planes on a Soviet merchant ship. On a regular basis Soviet Long Range Aviation and Soviet Naval Air Force aircraft probe the defenses of nearby countries. There are about three flights per month toward Norway, eight per month directed at Britain, seventeen per month in the vicinity of Japan, and numerous runs on other countries like Denmark and Sweden.

In the early 1960s Soviet planes began observing Western naval strike units, particularly U.S. and British aircraft carriers.[10] These sorties, which began in the Atlantic, became more frequent as the United States became more deeply involved in Vietnam. For a long while Soviet aircraft were unable to effectively monitor U.S. fleet activity in the Atlantic Ocean, however. This problem was solved when, in April 1970, Bear Ds began to reconnoiter off the U.S. East Coast, flying out of José Martí airfield in Havana.[11] They now conduct four to six flights a year. In December 1973 they began to fly South Atlantic patrols out of Conakry, Guinea, temporarily closing another large gap in the USSR's ocean surveillance.[12] Since 1971, Bears have intermittently patrolled over the Indian Ocean, after flying over Iran, presumably with the tacit approval of the shah.[13] More recently they have used Somalia to operate from. These missions provide the Soviet Indian Ocean naval squadron with air assistance it otherwise lacks.

The Indian Ocean reconnaissance stands in sharp contrast to missions flown over Iran itself. Beginning in 1973, MIG-25 Foxbats flying at high altitudes reportedly began to reconnoiter as far south as Teheran, flying some twenty missions in that year alone.[14] This activity was primarily an

9. Ibid., Sept. 10, 1948; Apr. 29 and 30, May 9, and Sept. 16, 1954; Mar. 17 and Apr. 27, 1959; Mar. 18, 1963; Sept. 17 and 25, 1964.

10. Norman Polmar, *Aircraft Carriers* (Doubleday, 1969), p. 662.

11. *Soviet Activities in Cuba,* pts. 6 and 7, *Communist Influence in the Western Hemisphere,* Hearings before the Subcommittee on International and Military Affairs of the House International Relations Committee, 94:1 and 2 (GPO, 1976), p. 7.

12. Ibid., Dec. 6, 1973. Recent reports indicate the Soviets are no longer using Conakry.

13. Norman Polmar, "Soviet Naval Aviation," *Air Force,* March 1976, p. 71.

14. *Aviation Week and Space Technology,* June 25, 1973, p. 11.

expression of concern over military buildup by a neighbor of the USSR and on the borders of a Soviet client, Iraq.

Of greater political concern has been the engagement of Soviet air force units or personnel in various conflicts in the Middle East, Africa, Asia, the Caribbean, and Eastern Europe. This activity is significant because it represents the commitment of an element of the Soviet armed forces to distant conflicts in which the risk of deeper involvement and wider conflict may be very real.

In the Korean War, Soviet pilots from both air-defense and tactical air units flew missions from North Korean airfields in aircraft with North Korean markings. Despite high losses in air-to-air combat and a rapid turnover in pilots, the Soviet air forces are believed to have gained much practical experience there.[15] In this same period, in 1951, Soviet air force units were deployed to Albania to intercept the few aircraft, flown by exiles, supporting anticommunist guerrillas in that country.[16]

In 1958, Soviet air force units may have been deployed to China during the Quemoy and Matsu crisis.[17] They were probably less deeply involved than in Korea, but again their dispatch was a demonstration of support for the host country and the experience they gained an incidental by-product.

Serious Soviet combat involvements began in the late 1960s. Late in 1967 the Soviets intervened in the Yemeni civil war, flying both transport missions and combat sorties in aircraft belonging to the republican forces.[18] Earlier in 1967, following the June War in the Middle East, Soviet Military Transport Aviation units staged through Yugoslavia began a large-scale effort to resupply the Arab forces. By the end of June, 130 jets had been delivered to Egypt and Syria. Interestingly, the majority of these replacements were MIG-17s rather than later-model MIG-21s.[19] The latter were not delivered for another year or two. Also during the June War there were reports that Soviet airborne units had been placed on alert. In October 1967, Soviet bombers made a courtesy visit to Egypt just after the sinking of an Israeli destroyer by Egyptian aircraft.[20] By the end of the year more than three thousand Soviet military

15. Letter to the author from Thomas W. Wolfe, Sept. 1, 1976, suggests that Soviet activity in the Korean War was useful.

16. *New York Times,* Mar. 31 and Dec. 28, 1951.

17. Ibid., Sept. 30, 1966.

18. Thomas W. Wolfe, *Soviet Power and Europe 1945–1970* (Johns Hopkins Press, 1970), p. 341. See also *Aviation Week and Space Technology,* June 1, 1970, p. 16.

19. Roger F. Pajak, "Soviet Arms and Egypt," *Survival,* vol. 17 (July–August 1975), p. 166.

20. *New York Times,* Dec. 4, 1967.

advisers were in Egypt, including a hundred pilots on duty with the Egyptian air force for training and exercises.[21] Over the same period, three hundred Egyptian pilots went to the USSR for training on MIG-21s, the mainstay of Frontal Aviation forces.[22]

The overriding reason for Soviet military interest in Egypt was to acquire facilities for the use of the growing Soviet naval squadron in the Mediterranean. The only practical way for the Soviet navy to counter the U.S. Sixth Fleet was to send some of its Northern Fleet submarines and Black Sea Fleet ships to the Mediterranean. For those ships, overseas bases were needed for repairs and resupply.

Soviet air forces, particularly Military Transport and Frontal Aviation, were used on a major scale in Eastern Europe for the first time in 1968. When the Soviet Union intervened in Czechoslovakia on August 28, the first units deployed were elements of an airborne division brought into Prague by 250 Military Transport aircraft.[23] These assault troops secured the airfield and all vital communication installations in the capital. They were supported, as was the whole operation, by aircraft used for "blanket" electronic jamming. Logistical support was later provided by both Soviet and Polish transport aircraft. The arrival of army ground units was protected by about 500 combat aircraft belonging to Warsaw Pact forces, more than 100 MIG-21s coming from Poland and 50 from East Germany, 50 Soviet YAK-28s from the 24th Tactical Air Army in East Germany, and some 100 MIG-21s and SU-7s from Hungary.[24] Other units in the western USSR were also on alert in case Czech resistance developed. As a result of the invasion of Czechoslovakia, a new group of Soviet forces was based in Eastern Europe, including elements of a new tactical air army.[25]

Soviet air forces have been used also for more peaceful activity in Europe. Frontal Aviation MIG-21 squadrons made state visits to Sweden in 1967[26] and to France in 1971. In the second visit, the chief of the air

21. Pajak, "Soviet Arms and Egypt," pp. 166–67.

22. *New York Times,* June 18, 1968.

23. Wolfe, *Soviet Power and Europe,* p. 469.

24. John Erickson, "MBFR: Force Levels and Security Requirements," *Strategic Review,* vol. 1 (Summer 1973), p. 35. The Soviet air army in East Germany since the 1950s had been identified as the 24th Air Army. It is now called the 16th Air Army, which was the designation of one of the air armies that defended Stalingrad in the early part of World War II and attacked Berlin at the end of the war.

25. Called Central Group of Forces with headquarters at Milovice, Czechoslovakia.

26. "Soviets in Sweden," *Flying Review International,* January 1968, p. 11. John F. Brindley, "Mig-21 ('Fishbed') Variants," *Aircraft Profile,* no. 238.

force, Marshal Pavel S. Kutakhov, went along. Both of these were seen as courtesy calls to promote better interstate relations.

But the most active political commitment of the Soviet air force continued in Egypt. The relationship between the USSR and Egypt changed markedly in 1970. From January to April, the Israeli air force flew twenty-seven to thirty sorties per day over the heartland of Egypt—the Nile Delta—in connection with the war of attrition then raging on the Suez Canal. The Israelis in that period dropped more than eight thousand tons of bombs, some on Cairo itself. The Egyptian air force was unable to stop the raids deep into Egypt. Pilots of its early-model MIG-21s could not match the Israeli Mirage 3s or F-4 Phantoms in combat, and Egypt's SA-2 Guideline missiles were useful only against planes flying at high altitudes. These problems were compounded by the Egyptians' loss of 150 pilots in air combat since 1967 and the destruction of many SA-2 sites.[27] The Soviet Union, facing a dual challenge to Nasser's political fortunes and its own prestige, acted decisively. Beginning in March of 1970, new low-altitude missiles (SA-3 Goas) were installed in Egypt and operated by Soviet personnel.[28] In April the first of 120–150 Soviet-piloted MIG-21 Fishbed Js—a much more capable model than the MIG-21s already in Egypt—began to arrive.[29] Though these aircraft belonged to Frontal Aviation, they were under the control of a PVO Strany general. There were also some reports that 30 SU-9s or SU-11s from the PVO Strany had been deployed to Egypt.[30] Soviet aircraft operated out of six Soviet-controlled airfields. The Soviet-operated air-defense system was intended to defend against penetrations of the Nile Delta and strikes at the Aswan Dam area, and to provide air cover for Egyptian fortifications on the west bank of the Suez Canal.[31]

Shortly after the MIG-21 Fishbed Js began to fly combat air patrols over Egypt, the Israelis stopped their deep raids.[32] Soviet patrols gradually

27. International Institute for Strategic Studies, "The Soviet Military Presence in the UAR," *Strategic Survey, 1970* (London: IISS, 1971), p. 46.

28. Pajak, "Soviet Arms and Egypt," p. 167.

29. IISS, "The Soviet Military Presence in the UAR," p. 49. See also Mohamed Heikal, *The Road to Ramadan* (New York: Times Newspapers, 1975), pp. 78–86.

30. Pajak, "Soviet Arms and Egypt," p. 167; William Beecher, *New York Times,* Sept. 1, 1971; and William Green and Gordon Swanborough, *The Observer's Aircraft Directory* (London: Frederick Warne, 1975), p. 208. Also in 1971 a brief appearance by PVO Strany SU-15 Flagons was reported.

31. IISS, "The Soviet Military Presence in the UAR," p. 49.

32. Pajak, "Soviet Arms and Egypt," p. 167. The last Israeli raid took place on Apr. 13, 1970.

flew closer to the canal until, late in July, an Israeli detachment deliberately ambushed a Soviet patrol and shot down five of the aircraft over the Nile Valley.[33] In response, rather than increasing their fighter force, the Soviets attempted to deny the skies to the Israeli air force by emphasizing ground-based air defenses and moving surface-to-air missile units closer to the canal. By the time of the cease-fire in August, Egypt had been turned into a "model" Soviet air-defense district. All early-warning and fire-control radars were operated by Soviet personnel, as well as the missile sites themselves.[34] And Soviet ships armed with surface-to-air missiles in Egyptian ports may also have been part of the air-defense system from time to time.

Later in 1970 and in 1971, new types of aircraft were deployed to Egypt, primarily for gathering intelligence. They included four MIG-25 Foxbat Bs, twelve TU-16 Badgers, and a small number of AN-12 Cub electronic intelligence aircraft (Elint), IL-38 Mays, and BE-12 Mails of the Soviet Naval Air Force.[35] The Foxbats were particularly active over the Sinai and along the Israeli coast. At least four flights were reported from October 1971 to May 1972.[36] The last MIG-25 flight occurred on May 16, while Soviet Defense Minister Andrei A. Grechko was in Cairo for talks on future shipments of weapons. The flight was commonly interpreted as a show of support for Egypt, in lieu of new weapons.[37]

Although these deployments secured the defense of the Egyptian heartland, they were not sufficient to prevent political relations between Egypt and the USSR from turning sour. Requests for new weapons such as the MIG-23 Flogger and MIG-25 Foxbat were turned down by the Soviet Union. For this and other reasons, in July of 1972 President Anwar Sadat asked that most of the seventeen thousand Soviet advisers in Egypt be removed. Along with the advisers went the aircraft and their pilots, and the Russians lost their six airfields. MIG-25 Foxbats, however, stayed on until October.[38]

The 1973 October War prompted a Soviet airlift of arms to Egypt and

33. Heikal, *The Road to Ramadan*, p. 164; and Laurence Whetten, "June 1967 to June 1971, Four Years of Canal War Reconsidered," *New Middle East*, June 1971, p. 23; see also *Aviation Week and Space Technology*, Apr. 19, 1971, p. 14.

34. Pajak, "Soviet Arms and Egypt," p. 168.

35. Ibid. It is believed that the AN-12 Cub Cs belonged to the navy.

36. *Aviation Week and Space Technology*, May 22, 1972, p. 21, and Apr. 19, 1971, p. 14.

37. Pajak, "Soviet Arms and Egypt," p. 169.

38. Up to forty-eight (at least thirty) Floggers were reported on delivery to Egypt though, beginning in February of 1975.

Table 4-2. Use of Soviet Air Forces as a Political Instrument in Areas Other than Egypt, 1971–76

Year	Location	Use	Aircraft used	Service component
1971	Sudan	Civil war aid	Helicopters	Military Transport Aviation
1971	Peru	Disaster relief	AN-22 Cock	Military Transport Aviation
1971	India	Aid in war with Pakistan	AN-12 Cub	Frontal Aviation
1973	Iraq	Arms transfer	TU-22 Blinder	Long Range Aviation
1973	Iraq	Aid in civil war with Kurds	Iraqi Floggers	Frontal Aviation
1974	Gulf of Suez	Minesweeping	MI-8 Hip	Naval Air Force
1974	Libya	Training operations	MIG-23 Flogger, TU-22 Blinder	Frontal Aviation, Long Range Aviation, Naval Air Force
1974	Cyprus	Airborne alert	AN-12 Cub, AN-22 Cock	Military Transport Aviation
1975	Somalia, Aden	Military exercise	IL-38 May, AN-12 Cub	Naval Air Force
1975	Syria	Reconnaissance	MIG-25 Foxbat	Frontal Aviation
1975–76	Angola	Civil war aid	AN-22, IL-76, Aeroflot IL-62	Military Transport Aviation

Sources: *New York Times*, Feb. 22, 1971, and Nov. 18, 1975; *Aviation Week and Space Technology*, Mar. 8, 1971, p. 27; *Washington Post*, Oct. 6, July 20, and Dec. 17, 1974; "Arab Air Power," *Air International*, vol. 13, no. 1 (July 1977), p. 7.

Syria of even greater proportions than that in 1967.[39] Early in the airlift there were sixty to ninety flights a day. Still, the Soviet airlift delivered only 15 million tons of matériel, compared to the U.S. airlift to Israel of 22.4 million tons. The USSR flew 930 missions, the United States only 567, carrying half again the tonnage of supplies the Soviet Union carried. And in terms of distance flown, the U.S. effort was four and a half times greater than the Soviet lift.

Also during the 1973 war the Russians threatened to intervene in Egypt with airborne units if the Israelis did not abide by the October 22 cease-fire.[40] Those threats were made credible when U.S. intelligence sources detected the diversion of Military Transport Aviation units from cargo flights to service in areas of the USSR where airborne units could be picked up.[41] But the Soviet units would have been no match for heavily armored Israeli units. Though the threat was a gesture of support for Egypt, it did little good for Soviet interests there in the long run. By May 1976 all Soviet military facilities in Egypt had been closed and relations between the two states were strained.

There were several minor involvements of the Soviet air forces in the Middle East and Africa during the 1970s (table 4-2), the most significant during the Angolan civil war in 1975 and 1976. During the last three months of 1975, Soviet AN-22s and IL-76s flew nearly forty missions in support of the Popular Movement for the Liberation of Angola (MPLA).[42] And in late January and early February 1976—the critical part of the war—Soviet planes were used to move Cuban troops to Angola since the United States had convinced other countries to deny Cuban aircraft the right to refuel. Fourteen flights by Aeroflot IL-62 Classics landed more than 2,500 Cuban soldiers.[43]

An even bolder combat commitment was made following the Angolan crisis. In April 1976, with Washington warning Cuba against any more overseas military involvements and indirectly threatening U.S. action against Cuba itself, the USSR deployed some twenty pilots from Frontal Aviation to help in training pilots for a squadron of Cuban MIG-21s.[44]

39. *Armed Forces Journal,* August 1974, p. 8.

40. Transcript of "CBS Reports: The Mysterious Alert," CBS Television Network, Jan. 17, 1974, p. 3.

41. For detailed descriptions of airborne preparations, see *Aviation Week and Space Technology,* Nov. 19, 1973, p. 14.

42. *New York Times,* Dec. 11, 1975, and Feb. 7, 1976.

43. *Baltimore Sun,* June 16, 1976; and *Newsweek,* Feb. 7, 1976, p. 38.

44. *Washington Star,* Apr. 6, 1976.

Whether coincidental or not, this ploy was a simple and low-cost way for the USSR to warn the United States that, if it did take action against Cuba, the Soviet Union would become involved.

The Soviet Union, over the years, has used its air forces as an instrument of foreign policy in different ways. It has used them more frequently and, in a sense, more deliberately and forcefully in recent years—particularly since the 1967 June War. All five of the Soviet air forces have participated, but use of each component has signaled a different sort of involvement—from a passive stance with Military Transport Aviation (except if carrying airborne forces), to a defensive stance with PVO Strany, to active and offensive roles with Frontal Aviation, Long Range Aviation, or the Soviet Naval Air Force. Thus the Soviet Union has demonstrated that air forces can be used as a political instrument whose psychological impact, quickness of response, and symbolic value as commitment to a host country's interest may exceed those of the navy, the service traditionally used for political operations.

Despite these political exercises, however, Soviet air forces have not had nearly as much combat service as U.S. air forces had in Korea and Vietnam. Indeed, as was the case in Egypt in 1970, when the Soviet air forces have confronted resistance in combat areas outside the Soviet Union, their response has been restrained. Only when there was no active opposition or direct threat of opposition have the Soviet air forces continued to prosecute their objectives.

Potential Wartime Roles

The potential roles of the Soviet air forces in wartime can only be envisioned in conjunction with those of the Soviet military apparatus as a whole. The prime concern of Soviet military power is the European theater, and it is here that Soviet equipment and doctrine would face their most stringent test.

In the event of war the tactical air force, Frontal Aviation, would be the component of the Soviet military that would first engage Western forces. The performance of Frontal Aviation, the most rapidly developing component of the Soviet air force, thus would constitute a critical test of Soviet power.

That test today would be much different from one ten to fifteen years ago. When tactical nuclear weapons were first given to Soviet theater forces around 1960, the Russians conceived of air power as mainly a defensive weapon. Western concepts then mainly envisioned air power as a means of striking with nuclear weapons at communication and transportation lines deep inside Warsaw Pact territory after establishing air supremacy in the theater. The Soviet Union's tactical fighters, with their short ranges, high fuel consumption, and light payloads, were inappropriate for nuclear strikes; their one advantage was their simple and rugged construction that would permit them to disperse in time of crisis to unimproved airfields, or even to grass strips, and perhaps survive.[45]

Thus, in the early 1960s, the Soviet air forces were mainly expected to defend targets in Eastern Europe, whether air bases, headquarters, or communication and transportation lines. The small and very maneuverable MIG-17s and MIG-21s were well-suited to their mission. Lacking search radar for long-range scanning, they were built to follow ground orders, which left their pilots little room for initiative.[46] Over the battle area itself, because they burned fuel so rapidly and had little endurance, the Soviet fighters would have had to be content with hit-and-run attacks against Western ground-attack planes, rather than contesting against fighters for air supremacy.

The shock tactics emphasized in Soviet doctrine in the early 1960s called for ground forces to advance rapidly to exploit preemptive strikes with nuclear and chemical weapons. Aircraft were expected to do little other than deter flanking counterattacks by Western European and U.S. divisions with nuclear weapons. If Western ground and air units slowed the Soviet advance, Warsaw Pact air units were to attempt to break the stalemate. Soviet aircraft would have been so inefficient at that task, however, that they probably could not have carried it out. The SU-7 Fitter, the standard ground-attack aircraft in the 1960s, flying over a nominal distance, could only deliver about one-fifth as heavy a payload as its replacement, the SU-17 Fitter C, could deliver today.[47]

The Russians' unhappiness with their lack of an alternative to the use

45. Roy M. Braybrook, "First Write Your Scenario . . . Then Choose Your Actors," *Air International,* December 1975, p. 295.

46. Search radars in the 1950s had a range of about 6 miles; in 1970, 50 miles. By 1980 it is likely to increase to 80 miles. Tracking radars initially had little more than a 2 mile range, but, by 1970 could track targets more than 12 miles away. By 1980 their range could triple. *International Defense Review,* vol. 9 (April 1976), p. 195.

47. *Fiscal Year 1977 Authorization for Military Procurement, Research and Development, and Active Duty, Selected Reserve and Civilian Personnel Strengths,* pt. 9, *Tactical Air Power,* Hearings before the Senate Armed Services Committee, 94:2 (GPO, 1976), p. 4751. A sketch in this source shows the SU-7 carrying two 250 kg bombs and the SU-17 carrying four 500 kg bombs plus two 250 kg bombs.

of chemical and nuclear weapons seems to have prompted their development of new weapon systems. Soviet aircraft in the early 1960s could only hope to defend rear operating areas briefly against air attack, and to provide minimal defense for land forces. Preemptive nuclear attacks at the very onset of hostilities, coupled with a quick occupation of Germany and Western Europe, were the only tactic that appeared to be viable. Nuclear devastation through surprise attack was expected to neutralize NATO tactical air power and nuclear weapons, the major threats to the Warsaw Pact countries. But this approach—grand in concept and attractive for the analyst—raised the prospect of Western nuclear retaliation on the USSR itself, not to mention a ravaged Europe. Options short of a nuclear free-for-all were needed so that a war in Europe might be ended before the losses outweighed the gains.

One change in military doctrine and force structure is reflected in the reequipment of Soviet ground forces that began in the mid-1960s. The new approach to warfare brought the introduction of mobile surface-to-air missiles, improved multibarrel rocket launchers, self-propelled artillery, a new main battle tank, and armored personnel carriers, plus increases in the number of artillery pieces and tanks in key divisions.[48] In effect, the ground forces absorbed aviation's traditional roles of air defense and close fire support. In this process the ground forces were protected by a bubble of antiair and ground-support firepower. The new equipment both magnified immensely the firepower of Soviet divisions and ensured that it would be in the right place when needed. Consequently, aircraft were freed for independent tasks, tasks still relevant to the ground battle but not directly tied to the movement of ground units. The equipment of tactical aviation has reflected the new freedom.

The family of tactical aircraft that have been entering service since about 1970 (SU-17, SU-19, MIG-23, and MIG-27) is quite different from earlier generations. These planes are heavier and larger than their predecessors. They can carry larger payloads over greater distances, and their avionic and jamming equipment are growing increasingly sophisticated.

---

48. At each Soviet army level there is an air defense group, presently equipped with four different types of antiaircraft guns and three different types of missiles. At each division level there are air-defense battalions with two different types of surface-to-air missiles and various caliber cannon. All told, there are more than 100 batteries of SA-2, SA-4, and SA-6s, probably over 1,000 SA-9 launchers, plus antiaircraft guns (ZSU-23/4, etc.), and more than 2,000 SA-7 hand-held SAM units in Eastern Europe. A new SAM, SA-8, was displayed in 1975 and is expected to enter service soon. Based on order of battle data in *International Defense Review,* vol. 7 (August 1974), p. 450.

Several of the new aircraft have swing wings which give the planes agility over a wide range of altitudes and speeds. The MIG-23 Flogger B has a radar whose range is equal to that of American aircraft of the mid-1960s like the F-4 Phantom. The SU-17 Fitter C, SU-19 Fencer, and MIG-27 Flogger D are all capable of carrying four precision-guided bombs.

The weapons the new aircraft carry have also been greatly improved. For air-to-air combat, MIG-23 Floggers now have the AA-7 Apex missile that has a range of nine to twenty miles and the AA-8 Aphid with a range of four to nine miles.[49] In these weapons some of the problems that limited the effectiveness of the earlier standard combat missile, the AA-2 Atoll, have presumably been eliminated.[50] There has been a tenfold increase in the range of missiles guided by radar and an eightfold increase in that of weapons with infrared guidance. From 1950 to 1970 the rate of fire of air-to-air cannons increased by over 125 percent, and it is expected to double again by 1980.[51]

In air-to-ground weaponry, new systems will soon replace the radio-commanded missiles such as the AS-7 Kerry. Four types of weapons, similar in lethality to U.S. precision munitions used in Vietnam and the Middle East, are under development. The AS-9 has a range of over fifty miles and is a radar-homing, antiradiation missile. The AS-10 is meant for use against sheltered targets; it is guided by an electro-optical system and can be fired at specific targets six miles away. Both are accurate when fired at targets from as low as 1,000–2,000 feet or as high as 15,000–25,000 feet. The AS-X, an advanced tactical missile, reportedly can be accurately fired at targets twenty-five miles away, uses electro-optical homing guidance with a data link for electro-optical command, and, most important, can be fired from some 500 feet above the ground.[52]

Frontal Aviation is no longer limited to reacting to ground develop-

49. The ranges depend on whether the missile is infrared- (short-range) or radar-guided. Soviet tactics indicate two missiles (one infrared-guided, one radar-guided) are to be fired at a target in *one pass,* so as to increase the probability of a hit despite countermeasures or an opportunity to "dog fight." See "World Missiles," *Flight International,* May 29, 1976, p. 1447.

50. "Both Sides of the Suez—Airpower in the Mid-East," *Aviation Week and Space Technology,* Special Issue, pp. 8 and 9. There is now an advanced Atoll in production with radar guidance.

51. Peter Bogart, "The Air Attack Potential of the Warsaw Pact," *International Defense Review,* vol. 9 (April 1976), p. 195.

52. General George S. Brown, "United States Military Posture for FY 1977" (Joint Chiefs of Staff, Jan. 20, 1976; processed), p. 66; *Aviation Week and Space Technology,* Jan. 24, 1977, p. 42. The AS-8 is an antitank missile that does not have to be tracked to its target. It has a range of five miles and is fired from attack helicopters.

Table 4-3. Number of Soviet and Eastern European Tactical Aircraft Available for Use in Central Europe, 1977[a]

Air force	Number of aircraft		
	In place[b]	Reinforcements	Total
Soviet	1,300	900[c]	2,200
Eastern Europe	590	0	590
Total	1,890	900	2,790

Sources: R. Meller, "Europe's New Generation of Combat Aircraft," *International Defense Review*, vol. 8 (April 1975), p. 177; and IISS, *The Military Balance 1977–1978*, pp. 13–15.

a. Soviet units not deemed available for use in Central Europe are the Southern Group of Forces (in Hungary) principally geared for Balkan operations, the Leningrad Military District deployed for Norwegian operations, and the Kiev and Odessa military districts designed for operations against the southern flank of NATO.

b. Forces in East Germany, Poland, and Czechoslovakia.

c. Forces in Baltic, Belorussian, and Carpathian military districts.

ments, as it was in the early 1960s; it can now initiate independent action as well. Low-flying planes armed with conventional weapons can be used against targets that formerly could be attacked only by intermediate-range ballistic missiles or high-altitude bombers carrying nuclear weapons because of the short range, small bomb load, and lack of avionics of older Soviet tactical aircraft.

In the opening phase of a war in Europe, Soviet and Warsaw Pact air forces would launch a large-scale attack on NATO air bases and nuclear storage areas in Central Europe. The total resources available for such an attack are shown in table 4-3. Coordinating a raid on all key NATO airfields before their planes could get off the ground would raise difficult problems. And such a raid would sap Soviet and Warsaw Pact air resources so that a second major attack would be almost impossible. Still, the initial onslaught could be devastating.

The Russians' new equipment may be an indication of a new approach to tactical nuclear warfare in Europe; perhaps to preserve the Soviet homeland from retaliatory attacks they have decided not to rely on the nuclear systems located there for tactical use. Frontal Aviation now has tactical aircraft deployed in Eastern Europe that could deliver tactical nuclear weapons against numerous targets in Western Europe. Whether this change is viewed in Soviet strategy as another firebreak in the European theater or as a new deterrent against NATO's first use of nuclear weapons is difficult to ascertain.[53]

53. For a more complete discussion of Soviet nuclear theater forces, see Joseph D. Douglass, Jr., *Studies in Communist Affairs*, vol. 1, *The Soviet Theatre Nuclear Offensive* (GPO, 1976), especially sec. 4c and pp. 112 and 117.

More important, the hardware developments seem to indicate that the Soviet Union may no longer plan for an inevitable rapid escalation to the use of nuclear weapons at the outset of war in Europe. This effort to raise the nuclear threshold does not imply that Soviet doctrine ensures that only conventional weapons would be used. The USSR remains prepared for the eventual use of nuclear weapons. But the forces built in the early 1960s for a short nuclear conflict have been modernized at considerable cost, and today the Russians, armed for the first time to fight a modern nonnuclear war, would not be compelled to immediately escalate to nuclear war. They may not choose to exercise the option, but they would at least have the choice of fighting a longer conventional-war phase.

Analyses of Soviet doctrine suggest that war in Europe for the USSR would probably be undertaken as part of a general war rather than be limited in area or intensity.[54] Soviet air forces in all likelihood would have to make the first thrust into NATO territory. The initial ground attacks on NATO targets by Soviet air regiments using conventional weapons would begin ten to fifteen minutes after Soviet aircraft left their bases in Eastern Europe, but they would be supported by bombers coming from the Soviet Union. In all its phases, the first air attack would last no more than six hours. A force of perhaps a thousand aircraft, with elements from Frontal Aviation, Long Range Aviation, and some Eastern European air forces, could be involved.

In the first echelon, a small number of aircraft would be used to clear corridors in the NATO air-defense system. The corridors would be narrow and deep enough only to destroy enemy missile-launching sites. This mission would include AN-12s and TU-16s for monitoring and jamming enemy radar, and SU-17, SU-19, and MIG-27 fighter-bombers armed with antiradar missiles (AS-9), antipersonnel weapons, and precision-guided missiles (AS-10) directed at enemy defenses. If NATO's interceptor aircraft reacted quickly enough to get into combat, MIG-23 Flogger Bs could be used to protect the Soviet strike force. Reconnaissance aircraft (MIG-21 and MIG-25) could be used to assess the damage.

Probably half of the total sorties in the first echelon would be flown by Frontal Aviation. And once they had crippled NATO's missile sites, these planes would be available for the initial conventional phase of the con-

54. See Secretary of Defense Donald H. Rumsfeld, "Annual Defense Department Report FY 1977" (Jan. 27, 1976; processed), pp. 125–26; *Fiscal Year 1977 Authorization*, pt. 9, *Tactical Air Power*, pp. 4848–54; and "Evolution in Air Defense Requirement," *International Defense Review*, vol. 7 (March 1974), p. 12.

flict. Frontal Aviation's primary area of responsibility would extend hundreds of miles into the theater. Moving through the cleared corridors, SU-17 Fitters, SU-19 Fencers, and MIG-27 Flogger Ds would fan out to strike at NATO airbases. A large number of aircraft (at least a regiment of thirty-six) using advanced munitions (AS-10, AS-X) would have to be committed to each air base if NATO shelters and aircraft were to be destroyed.[55] With a force of over a thousand aircraft, the most that could be expected would be the disruption and destruction of six to ten of NATO's bases. If each of these bases was assumed to support a minimum of one squadron, NATO losses might total 144 to 240 aircraft—the U.S. 17th Air Force has roughly 240 planes at its seven bases in Germany and the Netherlands. Fewer airfields would have to be included in the strike if command and control sites, like the one at Boerfink, and fixed and field storage sites for nuclear weapons were to be targets in the initial strike. Electronic jamming aircraft, such as the YAK-28 Brewer E, would screen the attacking force, and MIG-21, MIG-23, and MIG-F fighters would attempt to shield it from NATO air units.

The final echelon of the strike force would probably be assigned the smallest proportion of the total sorties flown. Aircraft assigned to Long Range Aviation would strike at air bases—particularly those in Britain—and storage sites for equipment for U.S. forces, nuclear storage sites, and headquarters areas outside of Frontal Aviation's operating radius, and at the extremes of the theater. Bombers such as the Backfire, TU-22 Blinder, and TU-16 Badger would hit at the deepest targets, using both standoff weapons and gravity bombs. Other Long Range aircraft would set up electronic jamming screens, and, in some instances, SU-19 Fencers could attack airfield defenses. Longer-range fighter aircraft, such as the MIG-23 Flogger B, could escort the older TU-16 Badgers while they were in the target areas.

In order to have a seriously debilitating effect on NATO air resources and nuclear options, the Soviet and Warsaw Pact air forces would have to have a large number of successes in a very short time. If a reasonable number of sorties were flown each day for five days, with a loss of 5–10 percent of the planes in each strike, about one-third of the attacking force would be lost. Even a force the size of the Soviet Union's would find it hard to replace such losses in a conventional conflict, and especially when general air operations will also have to be flown in support of ground

55. Carl Richard Neu, *Attacking Hardened Air Bases (AHAB): A Decision Analysis Aid for the Tactical Commander,* R-1422-PR (Rand Corp., 1974).

forces. Such losses might well be considered worth the risk, however, for the results expected.

In any case, Frontal Aviation, with its multiple responsibilities and its centralized maintenance facilities, and with an enemy that is prepared to counterattack, can only be counted on for a few major independent air operations at the outset of a war. But that may be all that would be required to quickly disrupt and even keep the U.S. air force, the most potent NATO air arm, on the ground and foreclose NATO's option to fall back on nuclear defenses. A doctrine aimed at achieving air supremacy through conventional preemptive air operations is the one for which Soviet air force will be most suited in the future.

The sorties not designated for the attack on air installations would be planned principally for use against a NATO ground force counterattack after a Soviet breakthrough. Their goal would be to secure the area that the ground armies were exploiting by attacking NATO forces moving into the battle area. Aircraft that are designed for use in independent operations could also be used in this role. They are ill suited for continuous ground-support missions, however. Thus the USSR is likely to develop a heavy-payload, low-performance aircraft as a supplement to the attack helicopter to ensure that ground forces have adequate firepower beyond the range of their own weapons.

Counter Plans for the West

Closing the skies to NATO aircraft at the forward edge of the battle area is now the responsibility of Soviet ground forces' mobile missile units. Thus, air combat is not likely to determine the results on the ground at the battlefront. And the firepower that fixed-wing aircraft were once expected to furnish front line troops is likely, in the future, to be provided more effectively by tanks, mechanized combat vehicles, multibarrel rocket launchers, and self-propelled artillery deployed with ground forces. Precision-guided antitank weapons already in the ground force arsenal will blunt the effectiveness of counterattacks. Also, attack helicopters and other aircraft operating behind the front lines will be able to provide fire support for stalled units or serve as buffers against enemy counterattacks.[56]

56. Philip A. Karber, "The Soviet Anti-Tank Debate," *Survival*, vol. 18 (May–June 1976), p. 105.

All of these developments, and especially the mobile surface-to-air missiles, will free Soviet Frontal Aviation for other, independent duties—in particular, to assure the mobility of ground forces by destroying Western aircraft on the ground.

Consequently, the West must take measures to protect those resources that are likely to be the primary targets of the initial Soviet air attacks: air bases, nuclear storage sites, and command and control centers. More weapon systems for air defense are needed; ways must be devised to repair runways rapidly; plans must be prepared to disperse aircraft, and a greater number of and more durable shelters must be built for aircraft and reserve stocks. Eventually, aircraft able to take off and land vertically or on short strips might be introduced so that they could operate from damaged runways. At the same time, NATO ground forces must assume that Soviet planning for a short war now envisions a conventional phase lasting days rather than hours; Western forces must prepare for a longer fight and for less tactical air support than now planned as some losses would no doubt result from the initial Soviet air attack despite the best preparations.

Aircraft Detection. Detection of low-flying intruders will be an increasingly important defense measure. Already, low-level, tactical surveillance radars have been distributed to the U.S. and West German armies. And introduction of airborne warning and control aircraft will give NATO commanders at least fifteen minutes' warning of an attack, more detail on the composition and targets of the attack, and a complete picture of the battle at all altitudes. If these aircraft work as well as they are supposed to, better use can then be made of other air and ground defenses. Western defense forces now spend much of their time trying to determine who is a friend and who a foe. The usefulness of long-range missiles, such as Sparrow, is limited because positive identification is needed before a missile is fired, especially in the kind of chaotic combat environment that would be found in Europe.[57] In past NATO exercises, estimates have been made that 40 percent of the NATO aircraft destroyed were victims of friendly forces.[58] The problem has been compounded in the 1970s because NATO's primary detection system, NADGE, is unable to detect low-flying aircraft of the type being introduced into Frontal Aviation. If the warning

57. In the Middle East war of 1973, 40 to 60 aircraft were battling each other at one time.

58. James Foley, "NATO's Achilles Heel: ECM," *Korea Herald,* Jan. 14, 1976, p. 4.

and control aircraft solves this problem alone, Western tactical aviation would be two to three times more efficient.

Air Superiority. NATO should continue to emphasize attaining limited air superiority, but that objective must be linked with an effort to knock out Soviet ground-based defenses. Contemporary Soviet military operations emphasize ground-based, mobile air defenses; it is doubtful, therefore, that even NATO's total supremacy against enemy aircraft over Europe would have a dominant influence on the initial ground battle. Air-to-air combat will continue to be significant, however, as a means of prohibiting enemy air action, particularly away from the front lines.

The question of how effective Soviet ground-based air defenses are going to be in countering Western close-air-support sorties is the crucial one. If Warsaw Pact air defenses overcame Western air offensives, they would eliminate what is now a very necessary source of firepower for NATO land forces. On the other hand, if NATO air forces were able to win this phase of the air battle in a short time with their F-4G Wild Weasels, antiradiation missiles, chaff-equipped aircraft, jamming pods on fighter-bombers, and new jamming systems such as EF-111s, NATO land forces probably could end the conventional phase of a war quickly. It is possible, of course, that neither side would gain a decisive edge and that Western land forces would have to face Soviet shock tactics with only a limited amount of close air support.[59]

59. Past wars provide little guidance. The U.S. air campaigns in both Korea and Vietnam had quite low loss rates (0.22 and 0.27 per 100 sorties, respectively), but they were staged against crude (though dense) air defenses. Against more sophisticated systems—for example, the SA-2 rings around Hanoi in December 1972—the losses were ten times as great (2.1 per 100 sorties). Yet, even these B-52 raids were challenged less directly than those that would be flown over Europe. Close-air-support losses in Europe would be closer to those inflicted on the Israelis in the October War of 1973 by forces whose equipment was similar in many respects to that found in Soviet forces today. Although total Israeli air force losses were 1.0 per 100 sorties, losses over the first four days were unexpectedly high: on the Egyptian front an average of 2.7, on the Syrian front an average of 5.7—nearly double what NATO expects its losses to be in close air support. Because the Israelis could not sustain such high loss rates, their air activity over the next two weeks focused on enemy defenses—in particular on missile sites (85 percent of the SAMs, both mobile and fixed, were destroyed, with about 90 percent of them eliminated by aircraft). This led to a reduction in the overall loss rate. Thus, the Israelis had uncontested control of the air and had won the "air battle" with an air-to-air kill ratio of 40:1. But with the Arab nations' fighters bedded down in base shelters or used for defense of their own air bases, and the time it took to destroy enemy defenses, air supremacy could not be properly exploited. The U.S. air force today, and certainly by 1985,

Ground-based Firepower. In order to continue as a viable force after a strong initial Soviet thrust, U.S. and NATO air forces will have to reduce their emphasis on providing direct support to ground forces on the front lines with multipurpose, fixed-wing aircraft. More specialized aircraft for close air support and greater firepower in the ground units themselves are the alternatives. Although there is reason, based on the Israeli air force's experience in the 1967 and 1973 Middle East wars, to doubt the effectiveness of low-level air support, artillery and ground-based rockets may suppress enemy defenses so effectively in future battles that some specialized close air support aircraft may be able to perform well against armor. In those past conflicts, multipurpose aircraft were more effective in destroying armored personnel carriers and supply trucks and in harassing troops outside the engagement area. Whether these targets should be considered important enough to justify the diversion of such highly capable and costly aircraft as the F-111 or Tornado would depend on whether specialized aircraft were available to provide close air support and how Soviet forces are employed in a conventional conflict. (Weather presents another problem, discussed in appendix B). In any event, like the Soviet ground forces, NATO ground forces are going to have to provide more of their own combat power at the battlefront.

Ground-based Defense Missiles. Although Soviet aircraft are not expected to concentrate on providing fire support at the front lines, ground-attack aircraft, including helicopters, will be used to attack NATO ground forces as they maneuver into position. To protect themselves against such a threat, NATO ground forces will have to be able to react quickly to attacks by Soviet aircraft flying at low and medium altitudes. A variety of surface-to-air missiles with multiple tracking modes and antiaircraft cannons, all mobile and capable of rapid, sustained rates of fire, would meet this need.

At present, U.S. forces in Germany have some 300 Chapparal and Vulcan gunfire units (useful only in good weather) and nearly 500 hand-held

---

should be able to do much better than the Israelis since it is far better equipped, trained, and prepared for electronic warfare and attack on enemy defenses than the Israelis were in 1973. See Charles W. Corddry, "The Yom Kippur War 1973, Lessons New and Old," *National Defense,* vol. 58 (May–June 1974), p. 508; Roy M. Braybrook, "Is It Goodbye to Ground Attack?" *Air International,* May 1976, p. 245; and Steven J. Rosen and Martin Indyk, "The Temptation to Pre-empt in a Fifth Arab-Israeli War," *Orbis,* vol. 20 (Summer 1976), p. 265.

Redeye infantry missile systems.[60] Redeye is also beginning to appear in Western European armies. Later systems, such as Stinger, could pick out targets over greater areas and in wider frequency bands than the Redeye. Much of the current NATO interest in surface-to-air missiles is directed toward the Roland, a mobile system for low-altitude air defense that would meet Western defense requirements.

IN ORDER to cope with the modern Soviet air and ground forces, U.S. and Western European armies eventually will need to be restructured and reequipped. NATO ground forces must acquire new equipment so that they will be able to fight independently of direct, low-level air support. Fortunately, NATO air forces can make use of existing and planned equipment; only modifications in doctrine and the use of its air forces are necessary if NATO is to prepare to cope successfully with Soviet air power and ensure that the air battles that are fought and won are relevant to the modern battlefield.

60. Based on estimates of U.S. Army Table of Organization, *Reference Book, Organizational Data for the Army in the Field,* USACGSC, RB 101-1 (Fort Leavenworth, Kan.: U.S. Army Command and General Staff College, 1970), p. 215; and IISS, *Military Balance 1976–1977,* pp. 5–7.

APPENDIX A

Soviet Aircraft Carriers

The Soviet Naval Air Force, much like the navy, has been innovative in adapting various technologies to suit its own needs.

The *Kiev* antisubmarine aircraft carrier, the first to carry fixed-wing aircraft, can accommodate an air regiment of twenty-five vertical takeoff and landing (VTOL) aircraft—the YAK-36 Forger—or about forty helicopters—the KA-25 Hormone.[1] In practice, however, it is likely to carry a balanced air regiment of twelve Forgers for air support and twenty Hormones mostly for antisubmarine warfare.[2] Ten Forgers, including a two-seat version, and fifteen Hormones were on the *Kiev* on its first deployment in July 1976.

The YAK-36 is a design developed from the Freehand, an experimental aircraft built by the Yakovlev design bureau in the mid-1960s. The Freehand was a single-seat, twin-turbojet, subsonic aircraft. Some twelve test prototypes were built. One prototype, seen in 1967, carried unguided air-to-ground rockets under its wings. In early 1973 the large antisubmarine cruiser, *Moskva,* undertook sea trials with a new VTOL aircraft, first flown in 1970. This was reportedly an earlier development of the Forger, referred to at the time as RAM-G.[3] It is believed that production of the Forger began in 1974.[4]

For every Soviet aircraft carrier built (estimates vary from at least three

1. *Fiscal Year 1976 and July–September 1976 Transition Period Authorization for Military Procurement, Research and Development, and Active Duty, Selected Reserve and Civilian Personnel Strengths,* pt. 3, *Manpower,* Hearings before the Senate Armed Services Committee, 94:1 (GPO, 1975), p. 3027.
2. *Aviation Week and Space Technology,* Sept. 6, 1976, p. 25.
3. *New York Times,* Feb. 27, 1973; and *Washington Star and News,* Apr. 26, 1973. The name is derived from Ramenskoye airfield southeast of Moscow where the new aircraft was also tested.
4. *Air Enthusiast International,* February 1974.

to perhaps six or more) the number of aircraft required could be about thirty. The small number of VTOL aircraft on the *Kiev* is not necessarily disadvantageous. The seventy to eighty aircraft assigned to U.S. carriers are needed when the primary mission is long-range reconnaissance, deep interdiction, or round-the-clock air defense of a fleet. But when the mission is local reconnaissance, dealing with minor air threats or limited surface threats, large numbers are not necessary.

The YAK-36 Forger or a follow-on will probably have a number of missions, including air neutralization through air combat, reconnaissance, surface attack, and antisubmarine warfare support. It would be ideally suited for intercepting Western patrol aircraft like the American P-3 Orion, Canadian Argus, and British Nimrod searching for Soviet strategic submarines, something that could not be done in the past. Air-to-air missiles such as the Aphid were seen on the *Kiev*'s deck. In addition, the helicopters on board could be used in a complementary protective role, defending Soviet strategic submarines being hunted by Western attack submarines. The Forger's reconnaissance missions would be focused on Western naval units in areas that land-based naval aviation cannot cover adequately. In surface attacks it could be used against Western naval units threatening Soviet submarines; it would be armed, preferably, with weapons of greater accuracy than the AS-7, so that payload requirements posed by the ordnance would be minimal. Strike power would be further increased when the Russians deploy electro-optical or antiradiation weapons (AS-9, AS-10, and AS-X). The Forger has also operated with air-to-surface munitions. The Forger could also help in antisubmarine warfare by dropping sonobuoys in areas reached most quickly by jets. Later Hormone As would be used in detecting the submarines.

The USSR has put considerable effort into developing the technology necessary for vertical and short takeoffs and landings (V/STOL). The Forger is probably similar in some performance aspects to the British Harrier; it has taken almost as long as the Harrier to be put into operational service (about nine years) and it is still in development. The Freehand was the only Soviet aircraft flown in the 1960s capable of vertical takeoff. The others under development were capable of only short takeoffs and landings. One was a modification of the MIG-21, called Fishbed G. The other two—the Faithless, built by Mikoyan, and the Flagon B, built by Sukhoi—used lift engines for takeoff and landing.[5]

5. *Flying Review International*, September 1967, p. 824.

Despite the *Kiev*'s 600-foot flight deck, both the launching and recovery of these planes present a problem due to limited deck space and deck-handling problems found even on aircraft carriers with arresting gear. Short takeoffs and landings are advantageous for extending range or increasing payload, but mostly for land-based aircraft operating from short grass strips and damaged airfields, where space is not so limited as it is on carriers.

Western V/STOL aircraft such as the Harrier have a great deal of versatility because of their sets of vectoring jet engine thrusters. The ability to rotate their engine nozzles gives them distinct advantages in combat and a wide choice in range and payload. The aircraft can decelerate rapidly, thus forcing opposing aircraft to overshoot. It also can turn in an extremely small radius and switch attitude rapidly, two maneuvers that also would spoil an attacking aircraft's aim. And rotating thrusters allow a short takeoff in which the aircraft's cargo of either fuel or weapons can be 20–25 percent heavier than in vertical takeoff.

But the YAK-36 Forger does not have this type of propulsion system, although it has swiveling rear nozzles. Its three engines, two for lift and one for cruise,[6] are believed to allow only vertical takeoffs and landings because it would encounter balance and thrust problems in conventional takeoffs and landings. Although it can operate easily from the *Kiev,* its combat skill and its range and payload will be far more limited than the Harrier's.

The *Kiev* improves the navy's combat capability, particularly in waters where its task is to protect Soviet strategic submarines in transit or on station.[7] Its air regiment, though now restricted in performance and in mission, will bolster antisubmarine operations in regional and distant waters and help other naval units broaden and improve their performance. Ultimately, if austere VTOL operations at sea prove effective, they could change the type of aircraft and air warfare over land later in this century.

6. *Flight International,* Sept. 18, 1976, p. 923.
7. For a discussion of these operations and their strategic implications, see Bradford Dismukes, "The Soviet Naval General Purpose Forces: Roles and Missions in Wartime" in Michael MccGwire and others, eds., *Soviet Naval Policy—Objectives and Constraints* (Praeger, 1975), pp. 573–600; and James McConnell, "The Gorshkov Articles, the New Gorshkov Book, and Their Relation to Policy" in Michael MccGwire and others, eds., *Soviet Naval Influences—Domestic and Foreign Dimensions* (Praeger, 1977), pp. 565–620.

European Weather

Weather in Europe, and over Germany in particular, can have a major effect on air battles. From flight training to the efficiency of precision-guided weapons, the importance of precipitation ceiling and visibility cannot be overrated (see table B-1). Daylight hours available for flying are also significant, especially for close-air-support flights.[1] During December in Central Europe there is a daily average of 7½ hours of daylight, and the average does not go above 9 hours from November through February. In contrast, it ranges from 14 hours to 17 hours from April through August.

Table B-1. Ceiling and Visibility Conditions in Europe and Germany
Percentage of days

	Ceiling (*feet*) and visibility (*miles*)					
	Less than 1,000 ft. and less than 3 mi.		Between 1,000 ft. and 3 mi. and 3,000 ft. and 3 mi.		More than 1,000 ft. and more than 3 mi.	
Months	*Europe*	*Germany*	*Europe*	*Germany*	*Europe*	*Germany*
January–March	33	28	21	27	46	45
April–June	10	8	16	16	74	76
July–September	10	11	16	15	74	74
October–December	34	35	26	27	40	38
December only	43	42	25	29	32	29

Source: *Close Air Support*, Hearings before the Special Subcommittee on Close Air Support of the Senate Armed Services Committee, 92:1 (GPO, 1971), p. 48.

1. Low-level flight training for NATO is a problem because of high population densities.

Table B-2. Number of All-weather Attack Aircraft in Air Force Inventories, 1977 and 1985

	Number available	
Aircraft	*1977*	*1985*
United States		
F-111	288	216
A-10	0	733
B-52D	80	80[a]
Western European NATO forces		
Tornado[b]	0	431
Buccaneer	56	50
Vulcan	50	a
USSR		
TU-16	305	100
TU-22	136	a
Backfire	35	350
SU-19	150	600

Source: Author's estimates and projections based on International Institute for Strategic Studies, *The Military Balance 1977–1978* (London: IISS, 1977); and "Military Aircraft of the World," *Flight International,* Mar. 3, 1977.

a. Number uncertain.

b. Not including 165 British air force interceptors, 113 German naval air force planes, and 100 Italian air force interceptors.

To offset these conditions, the United States is introducing precision navigation and location systems and developing special target-acquisition and -designation systems for long-range, standoff weapons. A sharp increase in the number of all-weather attack aircraft in 1980–85 (table B-2) will also help to ease the problem somewhat.